LANGUAGE AND LAUGHTER

CHOICE   OCT.'70

Speech. Theater & Dance

MILLS, John A. Language and Laughter; Comic Diction in the Plays of Bernard Shaw. Arizona, 1969. 176p bibl 68-9339. 6.50
This first highly disciplined analysis of "the relationship between Shaw's skill with words and his conspicuous ability to evoke laughter from audiences," takes its place next to Richard M. Ohmann's seminal study of Shaw's non dramatic prose, *Shaw: The Style and the Man* (1962), as an indispensable book on Shavian style. (F. Mayne's *The Wit and Satire of Bernard Shaw*, 1967, becomes an also-ran.) Mills examines precisely how Shaw uses such devices as dialect, linguistic satire, "automatism," and word-play (often wretched puns), as well as variations of his assertive, athletic "plain" style, to produce the comic effects he wants. Though Mills sometimes seems uncomfortable out of his restricted province — e.g. in his summary interpretations of *The Devil's Disciple* and *Pygmalion* — he is consistently acute doing his main business of elucidating Shaw's comic diction. His treatment of Burgess' dialect in *Candida* is brilliant, for instance, and his explanation of the nature of Tarleton's "instant information-retrieval" in *Misalliance* is superb. A badly edited book, the many typos at least do not mar its argument, and the spots of dissertationese are offset by its generally enviable style. Strongly recommended for all academic and many public libraries.

About the Author

JOHN A. MILLS dates his interest in Shaw from his high school days, when he chanced to read a clergyman's attack upon Shaw as a modern incarnation of the spirit of Antichrist. He has since acquainted himself with more moderate opinion on the meaning and value of Shaw's writing and has himself contributed to that opinion, in articles published in *The Shaw Review, The Quarterly Journal of Speech*, and *Drama Survey*. His knowledge of the plays may be credited greatly to his association with them as actor and director, first at Indiana University, where he took his Ph.D. in 1961, later at the University of Arizona where he taught and directed for five years, and later at the State University of New York at Binghamton, as assistant professor of Theater.

LANGUAGE AND LAUGHTER

*Comic Diction in the Plays
of
Bernard Shaw*

by John A. Mills

THE UNIVERSITY OF ARIZONA PRESS
TUCSON, ARIZONA

Permissions Gratefully Acknowledged

The Public Trustee and The Society of Authors, London, for quotations from the works of Bernard Shaw.

Sigmund Freud Copyrights Ltd., the Institute of Psycho-Analysis, Routledge & Kegan Paul Ltd., and the Hogarth Press Ltd., London; and W. W. Norton & Co., Inc., New York, for *Jokes and Their Relation to the Unconscious,* Vol. 8, Standard Edition of *The Complete Psychological Works of Sigmund Freud,* Tr. James Strachey, 1960.

Harcourt Brace & World, Inc., New York, for *The Misanthrope* by J.B.P. Molière. Tr. Richard Wilbur, copyright, 1955.

New Directions Publishing Corporation for *Bernard Shaw* by Eric Bentley, copyright, 1947.

Random House, Inc., New York, for *Portrait of Max* by S. N. Behrman, copyright, 1960.

Simon & Schuster, Inc., New York, for *The Enjoyment of Laughter* by Max Eastman, copyright, 1936.

World Publishing Co., Cleveland, Ohio, for *George Bernard Shaw: A Critical Survey,* edited by Louis Kronenberger. Copyright 1953, by the World Publishing Company, all rights reserved.

THE UNIVERSITY OF ARIZONA PRESS

Copyright © 1969
The Arizona Board of Regents
Library of Congress
Catalog Card No. 68-9339
Manufactured in the U.S.A.

To My Mother and Father

CONTENTS

FOREWORD

A few years ago, a production of Shaw's *Don Juan in Hell* which I directed was severely criticized by a reviewer for being "too funny." The complaint was that the actors — either at my bidding or with my permission — had interjected a spurious note of merriment into what should have been a predominately sober proceeding, *relieved* occasionally by a touch of comedy. The reviewer most likely had heard that the play, like Shaw's plays generally, was "intellectual," even "philosophical," and therefore concluded that these values obviously were being subverted in a production that evoked frequent laughter from the spectators.

Had our detractor been able to point to interpolated bits of horseplay, mugging, or outlandish costumes, he would have been on solid critical ground. But there was none of that. The actors sat on stools and read out Shaw's lines with intelligence, conviction, and zest — characterizing each of the speakers with as complete fidelity to the playwright's intentions as their talents allowed. Such delight as the audience experienced was in direct response, I remain convinced, to the materials Shaw set before them.

Does this mean that the play is *not* intellectual? The history of popular response to Shaw's dramatic works suggests that a great many people would say yes. Many who have found the plays richly amusing and have approved them on that score have been inclined to add: "Of course, they are essentially frivolous — delightful, to be sure, but lacking in real substance."

Behind such an attitude lies the erroneous assumption that if a work is comic it cannot, by that very fact, be of any genuine weight. This is simply the reverse of our reviewer's attitude, which was that the work in hand was of great intellectual import and could not, by that very fact, be comic.

To a certain extent, Shaw himself may be responsible for these conflicting and equally mistaken opinions. He repeatedly declared that his dramatic writing was essentially didactic and seemed to prove it by prefacing his plays with learned and lengthy expositions of their intent. In addition, he produced an impressive body of non-fiction dealing with questions of ethics, politics, economics, sociology, and a variety of other weighty topics — a phenomenon probably unparalleled in the work of other successful dramatists. In all of this, he presented the world with the image of a philosopher, an image which many readers and theatregoers find it difficult to banish even when the curtain goes up. Accordingly, this group comes to the plays with the conviction that they *must* be grave and ponderous works, given the character and the stated purposes of the man who wrote them.

At the same time, Shaw managed to appear before the world in the distinctly different role of the clown. In his letters to the editor, public appearances, and antics at social gatherings — as well as in numerous short theatre pieces of a wildly farcical nature — he established a reputation for irrepressible and irresponsible merry-making. The result has been that another large group comes to the plays for the laughs, without expectations of anything more substantial.

But though Shaw thus may have inadvertently fostered some of the confusion about the nature and value of his dramatic writing, the major cause of misinterpretation probably lies deeper. Those who regard Shaw as an important social and moral thinker and those who hail him as a skillful comic artist, are equally convinced that he could not — by the very nature of things — be both. The assumption in each instance is that comic effectiveness is fundamentally incompatible with intellectual substance. This is a rather common error, and one that has figured prominently in appraisals not only of Shaw's work but of comic writers generally. The attitude may well have come into existence as a reaction against centuries of critical theory which gave exaggerated emphasis to either the pleasurable or the "instructional" aspects of comedy. Critics who harped on comedy's didactic and morally edifying effects are probably most responsible. To turn from these writers with their talk of "amendment of lives" and "scourging of folly," to the palpable delights of the plays themselves, is to perceive a seemingly unbridgeable gap between theory and practice. Confronted with the evidence of the plays, the sensitive and intelligent reader has often felt compelled to reject all claims made for the seriousness of comedy.

The opinion of the anti-moralists has also seemed unacceptable to many. Dryden's contention, for example, that "the chief end of [comedy] is divertisement and delight; the business of the [comic] poet is to make you laugh," seems to belittle comedy, to leave out of account certain intellectual qualities which seem clearly present in plays by men like Dryden himself.

But to reject either the claim for delight or the claim for instruction, simply because one or the other has been overstated, is to defeat both purposes. The moralistic critics undoubtedly were injudicious in the importance they placed on comedy's ability to teach and correct; they also were somewhat mistaken in their understanding of how comic art achieved these laudable ends. But in perceiving, however dimly, that comedy can address itself to questions of vital human concern, that it can in short be serious, they were coming to grips with a truth which we can reject only at the risk of considerable damage to our understanding and appreciation of the art of comedy. Similarly, those who agreed with Dryden, though equally injudicious in the opposite direction, were basically sound in making pleasure a valid and important effect of comic literature.

Fortunately, the fact that a play can provoke both laughter and thought — not just alternately but simultaneously — has been much better understood by theorists of the last hundred years. These writers have come to recognize that delight and instruction do not, as had been supposed, occupy subordinate positions one to another, or even coordinate positions, but are in fact interlocking, interdependent, and inseparable.

In bare outline, the modern understanding of the matter is that laughter is the result of a special kind of purely intellectual activity on the part of the laugher. Comic laughter (as opposed to the laughter of hysteria or of sheer high spirits) is triggered by an intellectual perception, by mind-work, by an act of distinguishing and evaluating; it is thus the overt manifestation of a judgment passed on the thing laughed at.

One of the most eloquent and succinct statements of this concept was made by Ralph Waldo Emerson: "The presence of the ideal of right and of truth in all action makes the yawning delinquencies of practice remorseful to the conscience, tragic to the interest, but droll to the intellect. The activity of our sympathies may for a time hinder our perceiving the fact intellectually, and so deriving mirth from it; but all falsehoods, all vices seen at sufficient distance — seen from the point where our moral sympathies do not interfere — become ludicrous. The comedy is in the intellect's perception of discrepancy."

If this is true, then comedy achieves its seriousness not in the way that so many of the earlier writers seemed to say, not, that is, by the direct statement of principles of right conduct, not by direct exhortation to shun one set of manners and cling to another, but by the very act of presenting various forms of aberrant behavior for our amused contemplation. In this view, to have laughed is necessarily to have thought and judged, and the seriousness of comedy consists precisely in that activity.

But though all comedy is in this sense serious, there are of course degrees of seriousness. It matters very much what order of human eccentricity is presented for inspection and evaluation. To have perceived the discrepancy between running into a door and what Emerson would call "the ideal of right" which a successful exit would constitute, is to have functioned intellectually, but on a very low level of significance. But to have perceived the discrepancy between conventional views of marriage and "ideal" views, as Shaw invites us to do in *Don Juan in Hell,* and to have laughed at this "yawning delinquency," is to have engaged in a mental activity which may be assigned a high degree of seriousness.

The great comedies have always intermingled materials ranging from the lowest to the highest order, though they owe their preeminence to a primary concern with the latter. The plays of Bernard Shaw are no exception. This book deals with a variety of Shaw's comic materials, although they all belong to the same general category — the tendency of human beings to lapse from the ideal in their use of speech. Some of the examples treated occupy a rather modest position in the plays in which they appear. Others will be found to be organically related to Shaw's most substantial comic perceptions. All of the material is intended to contribute to an understanding of Shaw as a writer of plays which are at once richly comic and significantly intellectual.

Whatever value the book has will be largely attributable to Hubert Heffner, who suggested the topic to me and who equipped me with a large measure of such skill and knowledge as I have brought to it. I am also indebted to Lee Norvelle, Richard Moody, Raymond Smith, Gerhard Gaiser, Richard Scammon and Horst Frenz, who read the manuscript in its earliest form and contributed valuable suggestions. I want to thank Elizabeth Shaw for her intelligent editorial guidance, the University of Arizona Press for bringing the book into being, and my wife, for unwavering forbearance.

JOHN A. MILLS

LANGUAGE AND LAUGHTER

CHAPTER I

Introduction: *Words as Words*

"To me the whole vocabulary of English literature," Shaw *once declared, "from Shakespeare to the latest edition of the Encyclopaedia Britannica, is so completely and instantaneously at my call that I have never had to consult even a thesaurus except once or twice when for some reason I wanted a third or fourth synonym."*[1]

Though typically hyperbolic, the claim carries strong credibility. That Shaw was a stylist of formidable power, only his most vigorous detractors would offer to deny. John Gassner voices a widely accepted appraisal in calling Shaw "our greatest master of English prose since Dean Swift."[2]

In light of this, it is surprising that Shaw's way with words has received very little systematic, evaluatory analysis. As late as 1947, Eric Bentley could call Dixon Scott's essay on the subject, written some thirty years earlier, "the best of all descriptions of Shavian style."[3] Though incisive as far as it goes, Scott's brief inquiry treats no material from the plays and even predates such major works as *Heartbreak House* (1919), *Back to Methuselah* (1921), and *Saint Joan* (1924).[4]

Other commentary has been even more superficial, nearly all of it long on encomium and short on detailed investigation. J. B.

[*1*]

Priestly wrote that Shaw ". . . hammered out for himself a superb debating style, which was equally suitable for dramatic speech or polemical essays, and never too far from the stage or the platform; a style with a challenging and provocative tone in it, good enough for anything except dubieties and fine shades, in which its author had no interest."[5] Both in import and extent, the remark typifies the material available on this aspect of Shaw's work.

Not until 1962 did the subject attract the sustained attention of a scholar-critic. In that year, Richard M. Ohmann published *Shaw: The Style and The Man*, a thorough, lively and entirely persuasive account of Shaw's characteristic linguistic modes.[6]

Like Scott, however, Ohmann deals only with the non-dramatic prose. A number of important and very different questions remain to be answered about the language of the plays.

One such question has to do with the relationship between Shaw's skill with words and his conspicuous ability to evoke laughter from audiences. That he uses words with consummate artistry seems everywhere acknowledged; that his dramatic works afford a superlative degree of comic pleasure is also granted on all sides. But what, if anything, the two arts have to do with each other, has occasioned little comment. It is with this question that the present study will attempt to deal.

In order to make clear precisely what such an investigation will entail, a preliminary review of certain basic assumptions about the operation of language in drama seems essential. Considerable controversy surrounds this difficult topic, the chief combatants being the "new" critics on one side and the "Chicago" School, or Aristotelians, on the other. The position to be adopted here is frankly Aristotelian, and derives most particularly from the writings of Professor Elder Olson, a prominent member of the Chicago group.

In his celebrated attack on certain tenets of the new criticism, Olson summarizes the basic point of contention as follows:

The theories of [I. A.] Richards and [William] Empson illustrate a tendency, very prevalent among critics who rate diction as important, to rate it as entirely too important. In the order of our coming to know the poem, it is true, the words are all-important; without them we could not know the poem. But when we grasp the structure we see that in the poetic order they are the least important element; they are governed by everything else in the poem. We are in fact far less moved by the words as mere words than we think; we think ourselves moved mainly by them because they are the only visible or audible part of the poem.[7]

This tendency to misinterpret the function and hence overrate the effectiveness of diction has not been confined to critical theorists. Shaw himself was fond of remarking, by way of answer to the numerous critics who labeled his plays "talky," that his plays were indeed all words, just as Raphael's paintings were all paint.[8] By this he apparently meant that his detractors were foolish to condemn his plays for talkiness, since a dramatist can no more escape using words, i. e. "talk," than a painter can escape using paint — they are of the essence of his art.

The observation contains, of course, a kind of truth. That the dramatist must use words, only the most iconoclastic avant-gardist might refuse to grant. And yet, mere words, even if organized into meaningful discourse and spoken by characters, do not make drama, else we should expect to be treated to frequent performances of the dialogues of Plato. We are thus confronted with a seeming dilemma, in that the words of a play appear to be both the all of drama and yet not all.

The dilemma can be resolved only by reference to certain fundamental principles of dramatic structure. The ancient dictum to the effect that "the poet must be more the poet of his stories or plots than of his verses," takes us immediately to the heart of the matter. For as Aristotle makes clear elsewhere in the *Poetics,* words are only the means in which the dramatist imitates an object — that object being, as R. S. Crane describes it, "a particular temporal synthesis effected by the writer of the elements of action, character, and thought . . . ."[9] It is the apprehension and contemplation of this object, or plot, which constitute the primary source of poetic pleasure.

From this it follows that the words of a play produce most of their effects, not directly, as words, but indirectly, as the means of our coming to know the plot; most of the power of a play comes not from the words themselves but from what it is that they disclose. Accordingly, the effectiveness of words, *as words,* must be kept separate from the effectiveness of the elements of action, character, and thought which the words reveal.

Such a separation may at first seem mere sophistry, but its validity and importance become clearer upon a detailed consideration of the various elements which go to make up the poetic power of a line of dramatic dialogue.

To begin with the most complex case, a speech may produce an effect by virtue of its meaning, as modified or otherwise influenced by the precedent context and as productive of inference about action, character, or thought. Analysis of an example will show what is involved here. Macbeth's line, "The table's full," enjoys a much-deserved prestige for the profundity of its emotional impact. But an inquiry into the reasons for this power quickly reveals that it cannot be accounted for strictly in terms of its meaning. However ingenious, no amount of manipulation of the possible connotations and denotations of "table" or "full," and no amount of scrutiny of the syntactical laws of predication or attribution, will yield a sufficient cause for the proven power of the line.*

On the other hand, if the preceding context is brought to bear — Macbeth's character, Banquo's murder, the presence of Banquo at the table, and so forth, — the line takes on a significance far more powerful than was contained in the meaning of the verbal signs.

Part of the line's power, — the greater part in fact, — also stems from the inferences it allows us to make, inferences about Macbeth's state of mind, inferences which are no part of the line's meaning but which stem from the speech as action. As Olson argues, "What the poetic character says in the mimetic poem is speech and has meaning; his *saying it* is action, an act of persuading, confessing, commanding, informing, torturing, or what not."[10] Thus, once we have grasped the meaning of Macbeth's line, we infer that he has seen the ghost, that his mind rebels at the sight, and that he may reveal himself as Banquo's murderer, all of which causes us to fear for him, pity him, or react strongly in some similar fashion.

---

* The point is worth making, for as Olson has shown, Empson and others attempt to account for an effective line in precisely this fashion. ("William Empson," *passim*).

If this is true, it follows that words and their arrangement actually have little to do with the power of the line. It would be a mistake to praise the line as an example of fine diction, if such praise were meant to imply that the total effectiveness of the line depended on diction. Given the same preceding context, any words which conveyed the same meaning and thus permitted the same inferences would not be greatly inferior. Macbeth might have said, for example, "All the places are taken," or "There are no empty chairs," or something of the sort, without radically altering the emotional power of this precise moment in the play.

Most of the truly moving lines of a dramatic work will be found to be in this case; their power will be heavily dependent upon the reader's or spectator's knowledge of character and situation prior to the appearance of the line, and will be the resultant, primarily, of the inferences made about character and situation once the meaning of the line has been apprehended. By comparison, the words which make up the line, viewed simply as words, will be found to have little emotive significance.

Some lines take their special force not from the conjunction of all these components of effectiveness, but from the predominance of one or the other of them. For example, a line's power may reside almost exclusively in its meaning, preceding context and subsequent inference being of little or no moment. Horatio's celebrated "But look, the morn, in russet mantle clad, Walks o'er the dew on yon high eastward hill," is of this type. The pleasure the line affords depends scarcely at all upon knowledge of situation or character or upon implications of plot elements. It pleases simply as a happy idea. In other instances, the power of a line may depend primarily on knowledge of precedent context or upon the inferences it prompts about action to ensue.

* * *

In the light of these considerations, a distinction between the effectiveness of words themselves, and the effectiveness of what the words disclose may be accepted not only as valid but as essential. If the foregoing analysis is sound, it means that language, as such, can be assigned only a small part of the credit for the comic or tragic power of most dramatic speeches. Olson's statement of the case is admirably succinct; "the 'startling statement' in drama," he writes, "is startling because it discloses something startling, usually, not because it is startling as a matter of words and their arrangement . . . ." [11]

But "words and their arrangement" *can* of course be "startling" in themselves and are therefore a legitimate and important subject of study. The point here is not that word choice and syntax count for nothing; obviously, in the hands of a skillful dramatist they count heavily. The point is simply that a strictly stylistic study must concentrate on those effects which are truly attributable to words themselves, rather than to elements of plot and character revealed by the words. Such will be the method employed here.

Those effects which are attributable to words themselves may be said to be of two types, direct and indirect. Both require a word of explanation.

Direct effects are those which stem from the properties of words, as distinct from their meaning. The word "gut," for instance, is a short word, an Anglo-Saxon word, a harsh-sounding word and a colloquial word — all properties which have nothing to do with its meaning but which may nevertheless evoke a certain response. Thus, if a character in a play says, "My gut hurts," the word "gut" may produce a direct effect, an effect completely independent of the effect of the meaning of the line and the implications of the line as action. Depending upon the context, the fact of the character's complaining of an abdominal disorder may be extremely significant dramatically or may be simply indifferent. As a speech-act, the line may disclose much or little and hence be greatly effective or only mildly so. But whatever the significance of the line as revelatory of situation or character, the word "gut" will still have its particular power — a power which would vanish altogether upon the substitution of another word with the same meaning, provided that the word substituted had properties substantially different from those of the original word; "abdomen" would make quite a difference, "belly," not so much.

Similarly, syntax may evoke reactions separate from those evoked by the meaning and implications of the line as action. If a character says, for instance, "Throw your mother down the steps a broom," the very arrangement of words may produce its own special effect.

In Shaw's plays, these direct effects fall into four categories, each of which will be explored in subsequent chapters. Chapter III will examine Shaw's use of various dialects, especially cockney vocabulary and syntax. Chapter IV will treat the ways in which Shaw makes comic capital of various literary styles and of professional jargon. Chapter V will deal with the comic effectiveness of the repetition of words and of punning.

But though these materials will constitute the bulk of the study, attention will also be given to the indirect effectiveness of words as instruments of disclosure. To discover what is involved here, a further look at Macbeth's "The table's full" will be helpful. As already argued, the line moves us not so much as a matter of words possessed of certain properties but as a specific speech-act performed by a specially constituted character in a particular situation; this is so much the case that the greater part of the line's power remains even when a complete paraphrase is substituted, say, "All the places are taken." But it is immediately apparent that this paraphrase, like just about any other that might be concocted, fails to measure up to the original. The clear implication is that *some part* of the effect of Shakespeare's line, however minute, does depend upon word choice and arrangement. In short, the vocabulary and syntax of "The table's full" may be said to be indirectly productive of pleasure in that they possess properties which enhance the power of the line as a speech-act, such properties as concision, clarity, simplicity and familiarity.

In the same way, certain of Shaw's stylistic devices contribute to the comic impact of lines primarily comic for other reasons. This aspect of Shaw's dramatic prose will be the subject of Chapter VI.

One final point remains to be made. Studies of style inevitably raise questions about the degree of conscious artifice attributable to the artist. So long as the critic confines himself to an identification of those effects which a given piece of writing can be reasonably said to *have,* he is under no obligation to prove that the artist knowingly put them there. The "problem" is laid to rest once it is granted that the artist proceeds, in very large measure, at least, by intuition, and not by calculation.

Nevertheless, it seems prudent to try to restrict the discussion, in the present case, to those comic features of Shaw's style which appear to be the product of deliberate invention. Wherever possible, a case for deliberateness will be made, by reference either to relevant statements made by Shaw, or to the known facts of his artistic methods and purposes.

It also seems important to keep firmly in mind that Shaw was writing for the theatre. Hence, only those effects which could conceivably be operative in performance will be admitted to the discussion.

With this basis of procedure, it should be possible, other things being equal, to arrive at valid conclusions about the nature of the contribution language makes to the comic power of Shaw's plays. The distinctions made here will also facilitate determinations as to the importance and extent of this contribution, relative to other sources of comic effectiveness in the plays, since these distinctions indicate that drama, by its very nature, depends for its power upon something more than language as such.

To determine precisely what that "something more" is in Shaw's comedies, and thus make possible a more meaningful measurement of the contribution of language, it will be necessary to examine first Shaw's comic dramaturgy as a whole.

CHAPTER II

Shavian Comedy: The Major Aspects

Though no serious writer's works can be reduced to a formula, or even a series of formulas, close comparative study of an author's writing usually prompts certain generalizations about his way of looking at the world and about the techniques he has developed for representing that point of view. Such generalizations can serve a valuable purpose as a kind of critical shorthand, provided their special inadequacies in particular instances be borne firmly in mind.

Some such preliminary "position paper" seems particularly necessary in a study of a writer like Shaw, whose dramas have been subjected to a plethora of conflicting interpretation and evaluation. By now, of course, most of the earlier critical canards have been authoritatively overthrown, in the opinion of most serious students of his works, but among non-specialists certain half-truths and untruths still enjoy a nearly unquestioning acceptance. Thus, if the ensuing remarks sound to the Shaw scholar suspiciously like a vigorous assault on untenanted positions, the general reader may nevertheless find in them a helpful contour map of the Shavian literary terrain.

Shaw has himself supplied much important commentary on the implications of his work. In addition, various critics have addressed themselves to this task of generalization and have contributed enlightening observations. To ignore these and strike out afresh seems neither prudent nor necessary. A survey of Shaw's pertinent remarks, supplemented by the insights responsible criticism has thus far supplied, will yield the required information. Even so it will be necessary to develop certain points, qualify certain others and, in general, weld disconnected observations into a body of clear and related assumptions with an identifiable structure.

On one point nearly everyone agrees: Shaw played a key role in the development of a uniquely "modern" drama – a drama significantly different, not only from that of Shaw's own time, but from the drama of preceding ages. Hence, it may be well to begin with the question of what was *new* in Shavian dramaturgy, a question whose answer should also indicate what was old, or traditional.

When the American critics greeted Richard Mansfield's premiere production of *The Devil's Disciple* with excited commentary about its originality, Shaw answered that such commentary, ". . . if it applies to the incidents, plot, construction, and general professional and technical qualities of the play, is nonsense; for the truth is, I am in these matters a very old-fashioned playwright." *"The Devil's Disciple* has, in truth, a genuine novelty in it," he went on. "Only that novelty is not any invention of my own, but simply the novelty of the advanced thought of my day."[1]

Though Shaw had at this time – 1901 – written only ten plays, these revelations apply with equal validity to the greater part of his subsequent work. By and large, Shaw was, in structural matters, an old-fashioned playwright.

This may seem a curious statement to make about a man who has said: "I . . . have now, and have always had, an utter contempt for 'constructed' works of art,"[2] and who has also said, "I avoid plots like the plague . . . ."[3] But in a number of his other comments on play structure, Shaw revealed that he had something quite particular in mind when he spoke of plot – something which was actually not a matter of structure at all.

In *The Quintessence of Ibsenism,* he wrote: ". . . the rearrangement of haphazard facts into orderly and intelligent situations: these are both the oldest and the newest arts of the drama; and your plot construction and art of preparation are only the tricks of theatrical talent and the shifts of moral sterility . . . ."[4]

At first glance, this statement seems to offer little clarification of Shaw's view. Indeed, by praising "rearrangement" in the same breath in which he dismisses "preparation" and "plot construction," he seems to put himself in the indefensible position of accepting orthodox playcraft while in the very act of rejecting it, since "rearrangement" comes to much the same thing as "preparation" and "plot construction." But it should be noted that the statement contains certain qualitative terms; Shaw contrasts the arrangement of *"intelligent* situations," with "the shifts of *moral sterility. "* In these terms lie the real significance of the statement and a key to Shaw's true position.

For Shaw was never really opposed to structure — either in theory or practice — but only to that kind of structuring which he felt revealed "moral sterility" on the part of the playwright. Though he often called it "plot" or "construction," thereby obscuring the issue, what he really objected to was not the ordering of incidents, as such, but only the kind of ordering he found current in the popular drama of his time. The sort of manipulation he inveighed against under the misleading heading of "plot," was that which had for its basis, as he explained elsewhere, ". . . animal passion, sentimentally diluted . . . in conflict, not with real circumstances, but with a set of conventions and assumptions half of which do not exist off the stage, whilst the other half can either be evaded by a pretence of compliance or defied with complete impunity by any reasonably strong-minded person."[5]

In short, by "plot" Shaw meant only that kind of arranged stage action which had no basis in the "real" facts of human psychology and no relation to the "real" circumstances of human life. That he had no quarrel with the plotting of "real" circumstances, he clearly revealed in a preface to *Three Plays by Brieux.* ". . . It is the business of Brieux," he wrote, "to pick out the significant incidents from the chaos of daily happenings, and arrange them so that their relation to one another becomes significant . . . . This is the highest function that man can perform . . . ," he went on, "and this is why the great dramatists of the world . . . take that majestic and pontifical rank which seems so strangely above all the reasonable pretensions of mere strolling actors and theatrical authors."[6]

The kinds of plots produced by "mere . . . theatrical authors," Shaw often described, but perhaps nowhere more amusingly than in his account of why his own play, *Widowers' Houses,* failed with the critics. "The critics could not accept it as a play on any terms," he wrote, ". . . because its hero did not, when he learned that his income came from slum property, at once relinquish it (*i. e.*, make it a present to Sartorius without benefiting the tenants), and go to the goldfields to dig out nuggets with his strong right arm, so that he might return to wed his Blanche after a shipwreck (witnessed by her in a vision), just in time to rescue her from beggary, brought upon her by the discovery that Lickcheese was the rightful heir to the property of Sartorius, who had dispossessed and enslaved him by a series of forgeries unmasked by the faithful Cokane."[7]

It was against this sort of flummery that Shaw rebelled, not only in his critical writing but in the composition of his own plays. For the "conventions and assumptions" generating and binding together such incidents, Shaw substituted the "advanced thought" of his day. In that substitution lay a large part of the "new" element in his dramatic writing.

The innovation did not entail a rejection of all that was traditional. On the contrary, Shaw preserved not only the orthodox principle of arrangement, but in many instances incorporated in his plays even the stock incidents of popular drama. *The Devil's Disciple* represents a good example.

The play contains, as Shaw himself pointed out, all the time-tested materials of conventional melodrama: ". . . the reading of the will, the oppressed orphan finding a protector, the arrest, the heroic sacrifice, the court martial, the scaffold [and] the reprieve at the last moment."[8] But for the "conventional ethics and romantic logic" usually informing such events, Shaw substitutes what he called "natural history." Among other things, he has his protagonist make the usual heroic sacrifice for very unusual reasons. Rejecting the customary premise that "... a man or woman cannot be courageous and kind and friendly unless infatuatedly in love with somebody ...,"[9] Shaw has Dick Dudgeon offer his life for the life of the heroine's husband, not because he loves the heroine but because "the law of his own nature ... forbad him to cry out that the hangman's noose should be taken off his neck only to be put on another man's."[10]

The incorporation of this sort of character motivation seems only mildly novel today, but in 1897 it rendered the play virtually incomprehensible, even to literate playgoers. One critic of the time, unable to divorce himself from conventional thinking, concluded that Dick really was in love with Judith but was too much of a gentleman to say so, whereupon the actor playing Dick, having read the critic's review, promptly added to his business a fond kiss, thrown surreptitiously at Judith, to the great satisfaction of the audience.

By such departures as these Shaw created a drama sharply differentiated from the plays typical of his time. As Chesterton later observed, "Millions of melodramatic dramatists [had] made a man face death for the woman he loves; Shaw [made] him face death for the woman he does not love — merely in order to put woman in her place."[11]

But as suggested earlier, the new element in Shavian dramaturgy had a deeper significance than mere improvement upon Victorian melodrama. The qualities Shaw brought to his dramatic writing also set his work off from the serious drama of the past and gave it that character which has come to be called "modern."

* ❖ *

Shaw himself has often explained the nature of his break with the past, particularly in his numerous comparisons of his own work with that of Shakespeare. In one such explanation, he cites "morality" as the basic difference, describing his own as "original" and Shakespeare's as "ready-made," a "mere reach-me-down." Elaborating on this concept of morality, Shaw goes on to observe that the man in the street governs himself by "arbitrary rules of conduct, often frightfully destructive and in-human but at least definite rules enabling the common stupid man to know where he stands and what he may do and not do without getting into trouble." Shakespeare and others, says Shaw, accept this "ready-made morality," ". . . as the basis of all moral judgment and criticism of the characters they portray, even when their genius forces them to represent their most attractive heroes and heroines as violating the ready-made code in all directions." Shaw, on the other hand, regarding such rules as "no more invariably beneficial and respectable than the sunlight which ripens the wheat in Sussex and leaves the desert deadly in Sahara,"[12] substitutes instead an "original morality." Elsewhere, he generalizes about the nature of that morality and the impetus which lead him to seek it. "Caught," he writes, ". . . by the great wave of scientific enthusiasm . . . passing over Europe as a result of the discovery of Natural Selection by Darwin, and of the blow it dealt to the vulgar Bible-worship and redemption mongering which had hitherto passed among us for religion . . . , I wanted to get at the facts . . . to [establish] as the basis of [my] plays . . . not romance, but a really scientific history."[13]

Like so much of Shaw's writing, these remarks are "patently shrill here and deliberately shocking there — and somewhat glib throughout,"[14] but beneath the rhetorical persiflage lies a hard core of truth. Shaw identifies here one of the most important differences not only between himself and Shakespeare, but be-tween his brother modernists and the dramatists of earlier periods. Shakespeare, like pre-modern dramatists generally, could address his audience as priest, so to speak, in a celebration of communal conviction about the whole moral and intellectual life of man. Shaw characteristically appeared in the very different role of devil's disciple, heaping hot coals of disparagement on his auditors' most cherished beliefs.

Such a distinction may at first seem to flatter Shaw and denigrate Shakespeare, since it suggests that Shakespeare was merely conventional while Shaw was advanced and enlightened. But elsewhere Shaw speaks in a way that makes the distinction more palatable; he declares that there can never be "two Shakes-peares in one philosophic epoch, since . . . the first great comer in that epoch reaps the whole harvest and reduces those who come after to the rank of mere gleaners . . . ."[15] That is to say that Shakespeare gave the loftiest poetic expression to the great truths generally accepted, and rightly accepted, in his era. Shaw's idea here closely resembles Joseph Wood Krutch's contrast between the "classic" and the "revolutionary" writer, the former being one who "can take for granted the whole substratum of knowledge and belief, the whole system of values, by reference to which [his] story achieves its meaning," while the latter is a teller of stories "the intended significance of which [cannot] emerge unless the auditor [can] be made to revolutionize his moral and intellectual equipment."[16] As a congenitally revolutionary writer, Shaw turned away from the methods of the past and set himself the task of promulgating a new morality. Ignoring the valid moral and philosophic tenets of his era, he attacked the popular assumptions he believed had been invalidated, urging in their place the conclusions of the most advanced thought of his time. In this, he was doing something radically new.

But much the same thing might be said of Ibsen, Zola, Strindberg and other pioneers of modernism. To characterize Shavian drama in its particularity and thus set it off from the work of these writers, we need to consider the nature of Shaw's advanced thought and the form it takes in the plays.

According to Edmund Wilson, "The principal pattern which recurs in Bernard Shaw . . . is the polar opposition between the type of the saint and the type of the successful practical man. This conflict . . . is the principle of life of his plays. We find it in its clearest presentation in the opposition between Father Keegan and Tom Broadbent in *John Bull's Other Island* and between Major Barbara and Undershaft . . . ."[17]

Interpreted in the light of Shaw's own definition of "the type of the saint," Wilson's way of describing the plays has much to recommend it. In the preface to *Saint Joan,* Shaw explains that, for him, Joan's saintliness consists in her having acquired "new ideas . . . otherwise than by conscious ratiocination . . . ; " he equates the saint with the "type of the genius" whom he defines as "a person who, seeing farther and probing deeper than other people, has a different set of ethical valuations from theirs, and has energy enough to give effect to his extra vision and its valuations in whatever manner suits his or her specific talents."[18]

In the sense here given, all of Shaw's protagonists might be described as saints. They have a "set of ethical valuations" different from those of other people, valuations which they have acquired "otherwise than by conscious ratiocination." These protagonists Shaw surrounds with those "other people" he mentions, thus setting up the conflict which forms the basis of the dramatic action of his plays. Placed in a situation requiring action of some sort, the saint-genius responds in accordance with his "extra vision," while the other people offer more conventional reactions. The result is usually comic, though in some plays —*Saint Joan* for example — the protagonist's advanced ideas have painful consequences. But more typically, the saint provokes laughter by the eccentricity of his extra vision, while his antagonists arouse mirth by the blatancy of their conventionality. The saint, in short, makes witty analyses of the situation and the others' reaction to it, thus pointing up the humorous aspects of his antagonists' behavior.

The situations in which this activity occurs most often have to do with some aspect of modern social organization. Ronald Peacock has said that since Shaw's comedy flows from his criticism of society, "he needs for his purposes the ordinary social milieu, with the sort of crisis that arises from typical bourgeois circumstances."[19] Such a description works well enough for, say, *Major Barbara* and *Getting Married* but is something less than apt for *Caesar and Cleopatra* and *Saint Joan.* Nevertheless, whatever the specific physical setting of the action, the conflict between saint and practical man always has clear relevance to the contemporary scene. Modern social mores governing the relationship between the sexes make up the subject of disagreement in a great number of the plays, but contemporary ideas about social economics, jurisprudence, war, religion and government figure prominently as well.

Toward all such topics, Shaw's protagonists respond with "new ideas" and may, in that sense, be styled saints. But despite the warrant from the author, the use of such terminology has distinct disadvantages. Since Shaw's conception of saintliness differs so radically from the usual meaning of the term, ambiguity is almost inevitable. The average reader is apt to interpret "saint" in the usual, Christian sense and come to a false impression of the character of Shaw's writing, while even the reader who knows Shaw's connotation has always to lay aside his accustomed interpretations of the word.

Wilson himself, in fact, seems not to have escaped this confusion, for the major examples he cites are all characters who actually have some connection with religion, as normally understood. He seems to associate "saint" so closely with the practice of Christian religion, that he is forced to modify his first generalization in order to include plays which feature no parsons, Salvation-Army lasses, or the like. Thus he says ". . . these opposites [saint and practical man] have also a tendency to dissociate themselves from one another and to feature themselves sometimes, not correlatively, but alternatively in successive plays." *"Caesar and Cleopatra,"* he goes on to explain, "is a play that glorifies the practical man; [while] *Androcles and the Lion* is a play that glorifies the saint."[20]

Such a concession, it seems to me, all but invalidates the principle of "polar opposition" as a generalization about the plays. A formula which will not embrace so important a work as *Caesar* has little to recommend it, and the attempt to make it work by speaking of the two poles "featuring themselves . . . alternatively in successive plays" will hardly do. Surely the "principle of life" of *Caesar and Cleopatra* does not depend upon the presence of an "opposite pole" in *Androcles and the Lion* or some other play. Moreover, equating Tom Broadbent and Caesar as "practical men" and Major Barbara and Joan as "saints" can scarcely throw much light on the "principal pattern which recurs in Bernard Shaw." Surely Caesar has a great deal more in common with Joan than he has with Broadbent, while Barbara resembles Broadbent more than Joan.

It seems clear then that the application of the title of "saint" to Shaw's characters must be undertaken cautiously. Given Shaw's special meaning, the term accurately describes certain aspects of his protagonists, but confusion with Christian saint-liness seems inescapable and any attempt to make Christian saint-liness an essential element of Shavian dramaturgy can have little validity. A striking number of the major plays feature, it is true, important characters with more or less clearly defined religious connections, but to call these characters saints and thereby imply that they have a common quality essential in Shaw's scheme of things — a quality which puts them at the opposite pole from another group of characters who have no such religious connec-tions — is to misrepresent the basic organization of the plays.

* * *

A somewhat more satisfactory clue to the nature of that organization is to be found in those generalizations which describe the plays as conflicts between a realist and an idealist and/or Philistine. Since their introduction by Shaw in *The Quintessence of Ibsenism,* these terms have found frequent employment in analyses of his work. In his study of Shavian characterization, for example, Arthur H. Nethercot lays consid-erable stress on them, discussing a great number of Shaw's characters according as they belong to one or the other of these three classifications. Defending his commitment to this scheme, Nethercot asserts that ". . . in his second chapter [of the *Quintes-sence*] . . . Shaw lays the whole groundwork for his system." "These three types," he continues, "play . . . a significant role in Shaw's dramatic characterizations."[21]

In describing the three types and assigning them their respec-tive titles, Shaw asks the reader to "imagine a community of a thousand persons, organized for the perpetuation of the species on the basis of the British family . . . ."[22] Seven hundred of these citizens, Shaw claims, would settle comfortably into matrimony with never a thought about it, neither exalting it as the most beautiful of divinely sanctioned institutions nor deploring it as the crudest of human social expedients. These representatives of unquestioning contentment, Shaw styles "Philistines."

Another two hundred ninety-nine members of the group, Shaw continues, would find marriage in its unadorned essence intolerably utilitarian and would therefore proceed to beautify it by claiming divine sanction for it or by calling it the inevitable expression of pristine and inviolable natural law. These super-imposed embellishments Shaw labels "ideals," and scorns as "idealists" all who would make such claims.

The remaining member of the original group of one thousand, Shaw concludes, would say of marriage: "This thing is a failure for many of us . . . . Let us provide otherwise for the social ends which the family subserves, and then abolish its compulsory character altogether."[23] This last type Shaw styles the "realist."

That these observations provide an extremely useful tool for the analysis of Shaw's plays can scarcely be denied. With quite a fair amount of accuracy, Shaw's protagonists might be described as "realists," — men and women who face up to the truth, whether it be the truth of marriage or some other institution of modern society. Similarly, the antagonists in the plays may be meaningfully described as Philistines or idealists, men and women who either accept without question the status quo, or who mask reality with fancy pictures which they attempt to pawn off as the genuine article.

But the utility of such terms obviously depends entirely upon the troublesomely unorthodox meanings Shaw has assigned them. H. S. Duffin may sound a bit "schoolmasterish" when he agrees to use Shaw's terminology "without altogether assenting to its propriety," since "neither 'idealism' nor 'morality' in the senses given them by Shaw is recognized by the *New English Diction-ary*,"[24] but the built-in ambiguity of the terms remains a real stumbling-block nevertheless. To say of Shaw that he attacks "ideals" and "idealists" involves hazards of communication only partially compensated for by the sanction Shaw himself has given such usage.

But a more serious shortcoming of such terminology lies in the oversimplification it so readily prompts. Whatever the validity of calling a given Shaw protagonist a "realist," a full accounting of the character will always require much more than the affixing of a label. Speaking of *Candida,* whose three central characters have so often been forced into the realist-idealist-Philistine formula, Walter N. King offers students of the play the salutary reminder that "playgoers, who after all won for the play its first success and have continued to maintain its reputation ever since, do not react to *Candida* as if it were a geometry problem whose basic axioms can be located in *The Quintessence* and other Shaviana."[25] The point must be borne in mind wherever the terms are applied.

A third, and for present purposes final, way of looking at the basic scheme of Shaw's plays avoids the difficulties inherent in the two thus far considered, while incorporating most of the instructional value they contain and going substantially beyond it. Taking yet a different cue from Shaw's expository writing, Eric Bentley finds "the basis of Shavian comedy" in "the struggle between human vitality and artificial system." This struggle, he explains, "finds its chief manifestation in the struggle of the inner light of genuine conscience and healthy impulse against conventional ethics."[26]

This analysis has the great virtue of relating Shaw's dramatic writing to a central concept of Shavian thought — the concept of the Life Force, which Bentley refers to here as "vitality" and "healthy impulse." Summarizing Shaw's widely scattered remarks on this subject, philosopher C. E. M. Joad has explained the Life Force as follows:

Shaw postulates a universe containing or consisting of two factors, Life and matter . . . . Regarding matter in the light of an enemy, Life seeks to dominate and subdue it. Partly to this end, partly because of its innate drive to self-expression, Life enters into and animates matter. The product of this animation of matter by Life is a living organism . . . . Shaw suggests rather than explicitly states that Life cannot evolve or develop *unless* it enters into matter to create organisms; they are, in fact, the indispensable tools wherewith it promotes its own development. To put the point in another way, by means of the device of expressing itself in and through matter Life is enabled to enjoy a greater variety of experience, to accumulate more knowledge and greater intelligence and to develop a more intense power of awareness. To develop these faculties, to make these acquisitions may be described as Life's immediate purpose since they facilitate, indeed they constitute, the process of Life's development.[27]

In the struggle between vitality and artificial system which forms the basis of Shavian comedy, the characters who represent vitality or "healthy impulse," are those in whom Life is operating at full capacity, in whom Life is being allowed to "enjoy a greater variety of experience, to accumulate more knowledge and greater intelligence, and to develop a more intense power of awareness." They are instruments of a higher purpose, the purpose of Life itself.

But not all "living organisms" cooperate with Life. Some attempt to thwart its workings, either in themselves or others. In his essay on "Parents and Children," Shaw writes: "If you [parents] once allow yourself to regard a child as so much material for you to manufacture into any shape that happens to suit your fancy, you are defeating the experiment of the Life Force." "Most children," he goes on, "can be, and many are, hopelessly warped and wasted by parents who are ignorant and silly enough to suppose that they know what a human being ought tó be, and who stick at nothing in their determination to force their children into their moulds."[28] In the plays, those who thus thwart the Life Force are the proponents of "artificial system," and their natural opponents are the vitalists, constantly struggling against the imposition of "moulds."

* * *

This application of Shaw's theory of the Life Force to an analysis of his plays may seem unnecessarily metaphysical, but it helps to show, I think, the relation of his work to the mainstream of comic writing in general. Henri Bergson, whose concept of the *élan vital* so closely resembles Shaw's Life Force, finds the very essence of the comic in a struggle between "the living" and what he variously styles "automatism," "rigidity," and "inelasticity."[29] Similarly, John Palmer finds the head and source of the comic in the conflict between man's spiritual and animal natures,[30] a dichotomy which, like Bergson's, shows a clear similarity with the life-matter opposition found in Shaw's work.

An equally valuable adjunct of Bentley's analysis lies in the extension he makes of this basic principle of opposition. Equating the conflict of vitality and system with a struggle between "healthy impulse and conventional ethics," Bentley goes on to say that Shaw finds "the conventional ethics of modern life . . . to be identical with those of stage melodrama." "The stage, and particularly the late-Victorian stage," Bentley explains, "was apt to Shaw's purposes. He ridiculed the unreality of Victorian melodrama by letting in a flood of 'natural history.' But he found that the unreality was also real: the illusions of melodrama were precisely those which men fall victim to in 'real' life."[31]

This point of view finds expression in much of Shaw's critical writing. In the preface to *Three Plays for Puritans,* having inveighed at some length against "sentimental romances," Shaw concludes: "The worst of it is, that since man's intellectual consciousness of himself is derived from the descriptions of him in books, a persistent misrepresentation of humanity in literature gets finally accepted and acted upon."[32]

As this and similar passages make clear, Shaw perceived that the ethics of romantic fiction — especially as presented in stage melodrama — have a directly pernicious influence upon human conduct. Accordingly, in providing a social corrective through the medium of comedy, he chose to travesty stage ethics and thereby to ridicule not merely popular stage practice but actual social conduct. Observing that life tends to imitate art, he concluded that he could exert a salutary influence on life by providing a better object of imitation, while at the same time exposing the inadequacy of the usual models. This led him to organize his plays in a fashion which Bentley describes as "the inversion of melodrama."[33]

Some notion of what this process of inversion involves has already been put forward in the analysis of *The Devil's Disciple.* In this play, as we have seen, Shaw uses characters and situations borrowed from melodrama, but gives his hero a totally new motivation and mode of behavior. From what has been said about Shaw's concept of the Life Force and his view of the important relation between stage conduct and real human conduct, we can now interpret this innovation in more depth.

The hero, Dick Dudgeon, is one of Shaw's vitalists, a "living organism" in whom the higher purposes of Life are at work.

Surrounding this representative of "healthy impulse" are representatives of "artificial system" — Judith, Anderson, Dick's relatives, and Major Swindon. These characters, in contrast to Dick, behave in true melodrama fashion. They voice the sentiments, assume the postures and perform the actions of their non-Shavian stage counterparts. Judith, for instance, truly believes Dick loves her, any other motive for his proffered sacrifice being beyond her ken. Well schooled — through association with romantic fiction — in how to respond to such magnificent devotion, she promptly imagines herself in love with her benefactor, and proceeds to play her tragic role with every tear she can muster.

Hence, for a time, themselves unaware of Dick's true position, the spectators view the action with approximately the same hopes and fears as they might any other such tale of adventure. But in the end, Shaw thwarts the usual expectations, "inverting" the melodrama and exposing as absurd the interpretation which Judith, and the spectators, have placed upon Dick's action. Rescued from the scaffold, the hero does not fly to the arms of the heroine, nor does he play the even more thrilling role of concealing love for Judith in noble deference to her lawful husband. Instead, he gently but firmly spurns her, revealing that he does not love her and has never loved her. He has acted purely in response to healthy impulse. His ethics are those, not of the stage hero, but of a human being in whom the Life Force has developed to an advanced level of intelligence and humanity. He offers to die for Anderson not because he thinks him a better man and not because he loves his wife — not, in fact, for any conscious motive whatever. He does it in response to the loftiest impulse of which Life — unencumbered by superimposed mores — is capable: simple, selfless, natural goodness.

In this way Shaw depicts characters behaving in a fashion typical of the popular stage and, what is more important, typical of life itself, and exposes that behavior as ridiculous by contrasting it with conduct clearly more intelligent, more humane and, withal, more in harmony with the noblest pattern of living to which man can aspire.

* * *

But this is not to say that the play presents merely a static contrast of two types of characters. On the contrary, the clash of ideologies produces important changes in the hero's two chief antagonists. As a result of her encounter with Dick, Judith is "disillusioned;" as Bentley puts it, she "learns that she is really a wife and not an Isolde."[34] Similarly, Anderson is "converted;" responding, so to speak, to the Life Force, he learns that he is really a man of action, a man for whom the confinements of the ministry represent an imposition of artificial system upon his true nature. This process of change makes up the "inner action" of the play, while the working out of the story — arrest, conviction, preparations for hanging, etc. — forms the "outer action." The exploration of the psychology of the agents, with its attendant conflicts resulting in alterations of points of view, constitutes the specifically Shavian element — the element which Shaw injects into the melodrama framework, thereby inverting it.

To a greater or lesser extent, Shaw uses this device in all of his plays. Finding represented in melodrama the modes and motives of conduct he objected to in life, he developed the technique of criticising "unhealthy" social mores through a travesty of the literary form which, in his view, manufactured and promulgated them.

The device undergoes extensive variation from play to play, but the basic components are almost always discernible. In general, the plays vary on a continuum from maximum emphasis on the "outer action" to maximum emphasis on the "inner." In *The Devil's Disciple* the former predominates, perhaps more than in any other play. But *Arms and the Man, Candida, Caesar and Cleopatra,* and *Captain Brassbound's Conversion* also belong very near that end of the scale. *Man and Superman, John Bull's Other Island, Major Barbara, The Doctor's Dilemma, Pygmalion,* and *Saint Joan* may perhaps be placed somewhere near the middle. In these plays, a more or less melodramatic series of incidents remains near the forefront, but serves primarily as the occasion for psychological probing and ideological conflict on a much more extensive scale than in the other group of plays. Finally, at the other extreme, are the plays in which Shaw submerges — but does not dispense with — a conventional story line, placing major emphasis upon the inner action. *Getting Married, Misalliance, Heartbreak House, Back to Methuselah* and *The Apple Cart* belong to this class.*

But it matters little where a given play might appear on such a continuum; it is enough to notice that even the most ostensibly "actionless" plays preserve a substratum of melodramatic incident. Similarly, the plays display a significant uniformity in featuring characters easily recognizable as conventional stage types. Even so unorthodox a play as *Getting Married* employs a company composed of the two ingénues, a stuffy British general fresh from India, a cranky old maid, a gay divorcee, a low-comic tradesman, and others.

More important than any of these features is the regular recurrence of the basic conflict between vitality and convention, with the latter taking the form of melodramatic protestations about "duty," "honor," "the sanctity of the home," "the dignity of simple poverty," and so on — sometimes accompanied by corresponding decisions and actions, sometimes not. Attendant changes in the outlook of the major spokesmen for system, brought about by the catalytic agency of the vital character, occur with equal regularity. Thus Chesterton could say of *Arms and the Man* that *"like nearly all* Shaw's plays, [it is] the dialogue of a conversion."[35]

This way of looking at the plays provides a valid and serviceable set of generalizations about Shaw's extensive and widely varied dramatic output. It shows the important elements common to all the plays while at the same time providing an instrument for a rather profound probing of individual works. In addition, it relates the plays to the major tendencies of Shaw's thinking, as revealed in his non-dramatic writing, while also showing the relation between the materials Shaw works with and those of the greater portion of the drama of his contemporaries.

But this is not to say that Bentley's approach, as summarized and in some ways expanded here, renders superfluous other

---

* Bentley offers no such breakdown into classes, but his remarks, I think, justify it. This grouping, including only the major plays, is meant to be merely suggestive. Roughly chronological, it indicates a progression from strong outer action in the early plays to strong inner action in the later ones, with occasional throwbacks.

attempts to find a unity of essential elements in the plays. On the contrary, the concept of the saint-genius and the realist-idealist scheme of interpretation provide valuable supplementary insights which will be called into play in the ensuing analysis.

Nor are these generalizations to be considered exhaustive, even as generalizations. A full accounting of the important aspects the plays hold in common would have to include much more than has been attempted here. But as Jacques Barzun has said, "Ideally, the wide world in the artist's mind is not to be inventoried, even when the mind is a far narrower one than Shaw's. The best record of it is in the author's own hand . . . ."[36] An attempt at inventory seemed imperative here, but it remains necessarily partial.

A final point perhaps requires consideration. In view of all that has been said, it should be clear that the primary source of comic power in Shaw's plays is the thought exhibited by the characters in them. The clash of dissimilar ideologies, so essential in Shavian dramaturgy, produces the major portion of the comic pleasure the plays afford. Hence, in identifying and evaluating the ways in which Shaw uses words for comic effectiveness, we shall necessarily be dealing with devices of relatively little weight, measured against other comic elements at work in the plays.

But attention to minor details can be of considerable importance to criticism, in so far as an artist's handling of such details may reveal the depth, or lack of depth, of his artistic resources. The work of great artists, abounds in subtle strokes which supplement and enhance the effects of the more obvious beauties. It is with such strokes that the following chapters will deal.

CHAPTER III

Dialect and Comic Effect

Though the use of "low" speech in the delineation of serious dramatic characters is a comparatively modern phenomenon, the diction of the street and the barnyard has figured prominently in comic characterization since the very beginning of the dramatic form. A natural concomitant of the village revels out of which comedy grew, the device persisted even when more sophisticated minds emerged to mold traditional comic materials into a fully articulated literary genre. Aristophanes' soldiers and rustics employ an idiom clearly rooted in natural speech, and colloquialism contributes substantially to the comic power of the plays of Plautus and Terence.

The earliest examples of English comedy also exhibit a decided bias in favor of workaday speech. Mak the sheep-stealer, of *The Second Shepherd's Play,* talks in the idiom of his station and profession and the natural dialogue of John Heywood's interludes continues the tradition. *Ralph Roister Doister* abounds in realistic detail, and *Gammer Gurton's Needle* fairly crackles with the linguistic exuberance of rustic speech.

With Gascoigne's translation of Ariosto's *I Suppositi,* in 1566, realism fuses with prose to further advance comedy's traditional alliance with the speech of the real world.[1] Prose of a similar caste, peppered with the epithets of market-place and alehouse, enlivens the comic scenes of the early Elizabethan chronicles.

Later Elizabethan dramatists quickly improved upon these first fumbling efforts, hammering out a prose style of great flexibility and subtlety, shot through with the jigging, bounding heartiness, and lively spontaneity of the spoken word. Lodge and Greene added incisiveness and coherence, clearing ground for the full flowering of the low comic idiom in the mouths of Shakespeare's rude mechanicals.

In Shakespeare's plays, the loose-jointed cacophonies of the vernacular remain tangential to other blocks of language: the vaulting lyricism of blank verse and the ordered harmonies of a more refined prose. Ben Jonson, on the other hand, elevates realistic representation of the language of common life to a first principle of construction, making the device a primary source of the comic power of his plays.[2] His work marks an apotheosis of comedy's ancient courtship of dialect and the common idiom.

Since Jonson, the device has retained a place in the storehouse of comic machinery, but has been used most often for secondary effects, somewhat in the manner of Shakespeare. Restoration plays feature a number of bumpkins and louts who now and again flavor the air with the pungencies of primitive utterance, but for the most part, Congreve and his colleagues favor other materials. Similarly, Sheridan and Goldsmith know how to dress out a low character in suitably picturesque linguistic plumage, but other devices claim the bulk of their attention.

Comedy-melodrama of the nineteenth century — both British and American — makes wide use of low speech, especially dialects, but when comedy of manners returns to the stage we find Oscar Wilde, not surprisingly, eschewing the device altogether. Coward, Behrman, and their contemporaries are somewhat less disdainful but also use the vulgarisms of the working classes rather sparingly.

Thus, throughout the history of the comic form, dramatists have made frequent use of the language of low characters.* This is

---

* It might be more accurate to say that comedy has frequently focused upon low characters, with the language simply following as a natural requirement of realistic characterization. But the language remains a source of delight, regardless of how it evolved.

not to say, however, that the device serves always the same function. On the contrary, at least three general classes of effects may be distinguished.

In many instances, perhaps most, the spectator is merely invited to enjoy the gusto and rich expressiveness of vulgar speech as a thing of beauty in itself — as a kind of back-parlor poetry capable of achieving effects denied to a more refined idiom. As Jonas Barish says, "The craving for a dramatic speech with sap and savor in it is as perennial as any other desire with which audiences have wedged themselves, century after century, into box, pit, or gallery." "Good realistic dialogue," he continues, "releases the expressive voltage, finds definitive form for that aspect of our sensibility — wherever one locates it — commonly denoted as 'low'."[3] The verbal gymnastics of Plautus' running slaves belong to this class, as do the linguistic gambols of Shakespeare's drawers and draymen and Synge's Aran Islanders. Assonance and alliteration, pleonasm and periphrasis, ellipsis and solecism — to name only a few of the devices — combine to reproduce the quicksilver verve of live talk. The effect is somewhat akin to that produced by the swat and the pratfall; we exult in the display of sheer animal spirits.

But vernacular speech, artfully manipulated, may also represent a more or less pronounced deviation from the linguistic norm of a given audience; it may embody a quality of quaintness capable of touching off the primordial comic response to what Aristotle called the "non-painful bad." By broadening and extending the natural peculiarities of untutored grammar, syntax, and vocabulary, the comic dramatist can concoct a mode of utterance, still recognizable as realistic, but laughable for its abnormality. Here the antic strangeness of the verbal trappings provokes mirth, just as peculiarities of physiognomy or dress often do.

Finally, low speech may be ordered so as to serve as an objective correlative of other comic aspects of character. Thus, a marked penchant for the crude and salacious in words may bespeak a disposition inclined to dwell upon such matters. Or, displayed often enough, the inability to speak in a connected fashion may point to a disturbance more fundamental. Here the language evokes a comic response not merely by virtue of its color or peculiarity, as in the other two categories, but as an explicit index of character, paralleling and reinforcing the non-verbal activity of the agent.

In the plays of Bernard Shaw, low speech operates on all three of these levels; it assumes its most conspicuous form in the cockney dialect of a number of characters in both major and minor plays.

In reproducing the authentic dialect orthographically, Shaw was adopting a relatively new device. Julian Franklyn cites Henry Fielding as the first to attempt it and credits Dickens with popularizing the technique, especially through his characterization of Sam Weller.[4] *Punch* took Dickens for a model and preserved the tradition "almost without any alterations whatever,"[5] until the early eighties of the past century. In that decade, as Shaw himself reports, "Andrew Tuer called attention in the *Pall Mall Gazette* to several peculiarities of modern cockney, and to the obsolescence of the Dickens dialect that was still being copied from book to book by authors who never dreamt of using their ears, much less of training them to listen."[6] In 1890, Tuer published *Thenks Awf'lly,* a full-scale rendering of cockney which may have served Shaw as a model in his characterization of Felix Drinkwater.[7]

Shaw's own interest in the phonetic oddities of London working-class speech dates from the time of his first exposure to it. "When I first came to London in 1876," he explains, "the Sam Weller dialect had passed away so completely that I should have given it up as a literary fiction if I had not discovered it surviving in a Middlesex village, and heard of it from an Essex one."[8] The interest first found literary expression in his early novel, *Love Among The Artists* (1881), where Shaw has his hero, Owen Jack, laboring mightily to correct the street diction of the would-be actress Magdalen Brailsford.

Shaw's first play, *Widowers' Houses* (1892), also has a cockney character, in Sartorius' scrofulous collector of rents — Lickcheese. At least he seems to be a cockney; Shaw never calls him that but he certainly hails from the lowest London class and his speech has at least a smattering of the familiar dialectal elements. He drops his "h's" and terminal consonants, though only occasionally, has trouble with polysyllables ("sekketery") and employs at least a few colorful colloquialisms ("dooty's another pair o' shoes"). But more often than not, his speech, though always crude, contains only a hint of the full-blooded dialect: "Oh come, Sartorius! don't talk as if you was the only father in the world. I have a daughter too; and my feelins in that matter is just as fine as yours. I propose nothing but what is for Miss Blanche's advantage and Dr. Trench's."*

The result is that Lickcheese's use of the language calls very little attention to itself, and that is no doubt precisely what Shaw intends. For however it may be in real life, in the mouth of a fictional character, the more extreme forms of low speech, particularly an idiom as bizarre as cockney, are inherently comic. Such speech will, therefore, not work well for a character designed to provoke strong antipathy; Lickcheese is such a character, and Shaw accordingly underplays the dialect in delineating him.

Shaw's first comic use of the dialect came three years and three plays later, in the speech of Burgess, Candida's father. Burgess, whom Louis Kronenberger has described as "orthodox low comedy," owes a considerable portion of his comic power to his peculiarities of utterance, peculiarities which resemble but far outnumber those given to Lickcheese. In general, his deviations from standard English phonetics follow the patterns established by Dickens, Tuer and others.[9] The aberrations most frequently employed include:

I. Misplacement of "h."
    A. Adding; as in: "hever" for "ever," "hold" for "old," "howned" for "owned," etc.
    B. Pronouncing initial silent "h," indicated typographically by italics; e.g.: "*h*our," "*h*onest," "*h*onourable."
    C. Dropping "h."
        1. Initially; as in " 'as" for "has," " 'ands" for "hands," etc.
        2. Internally; as in: "be'ind" for "behind," "fat'ead" for "fathead," and "be'ave" for "behave."

---

* The nature of the analysis requires such extensive quoting, not only of speeches but of single words and phrases, that I have omitted citation of page numbers in quoting from the plays. With a few exceptions, noted where they occur, all quotations from the plays are from the Standard Edition, London: Constable, 1931.

II. Dropping of terminal consonant; e.g.: "spoilin," "mornin," "contrac."
III. Transposition of consonants; e.g.: "scounderl," and "potery" for "poetry."

Such curiosities, representing a rather considerable degree of linguistic malfeasance, evince at least a modicum of comic pleasure. As Max Eastman says, ". . . distortions of our speech patterns are intrinsically funny when plausibly introduced, and the function of the ignorant character is usually to introduce them plausibly." "In the permanent condition called mirth," he continues," . . . distorted things are funny — and words sometimes the funniest of all. Everybody who has been a child, or been in a laughing fit, knows this."[10] Burgess' articulatory distortions scarcely provoke laughing fits, but they do provide that primitive delight in the bizarre, mentioned earlier as the second class of effects produced by low speech.

Burgess' mode of utterance also provides amusement by virtue of its liveliness and rich expressiveness. Such words and phrases as "garn," "sacked," "queer bird," "bit of a flat," and "devil a better" have a special saltiness capable of engendering reactions at least akin to the comic. The sap and savor of "curse 'em for a parcel o' meddlin' fools," has such an effect, to say nothing of a verbal romp like: "James is receivin' a deppitation in the dinin' room; and Candy is hupstairs educatin' of a young stitcher gurl she's hinterested in."

These and similar linguistic features though at least mildly mirth-provoking, occur simply as the natural concomitants of the dialect. Realistic representation of cockney speech necessarily includes such elements. Hence, such amusement as they provide remains, in a sense, an accident of construction, rather than an effect consciously and deliberately produced. In another sense, of course, the effect may be called deliberate, in that the playwright, in creating the character and rendering his speech realistically, could hardly have been ignorant of the comic potentialities of such speech. But since any reasonably accurate representation of the dialect would have the same characteristics and the same comic potential, these features of Burgess' speech reveal very little in the way of distinctively individual comic inventiveness on Shaw's part. They reveal only accurate transcription of a real mode of utterance which happens to possess certain comic aspects.

But Shaw does go beyond mere verisimilitude in his delineation of Burgess' mode of utterance. In a significant number of instances, he seems to select, shape, and order words so as to achieve comic effects not simply inherent in the dialect.

Thus, on a number of occasions, the natural vulgarities of Burgess' speech style stand in comic juxtaposition to more refined elements in his style; while trying to achieve a certain elegance of expression, Burgess plunges incongruously into solecism. Of his *bête noire,* Prossy, for example, he declaims haughtily: "I wouldn't demean myself to take notice on her." The substitution of "on" for "of," coming close upon the heels of the well-turned "demean myself" produces somewhat the same effect as the sight of a man in formal dress slipping on a banana peel. The fact that Burgess uses the correct idiom, "notice of," just a few lines earlier, seems to argue for deliberate comic design here. With Lexy he assays a similar air of superiority, with approximately the same result. "Don't let me detain you, Mr. Mill," he announces — "momentously," according to Shaw's stage direction. "What I come about is private between me and Mr. Morell."

Other attempts at fineness of phrase prove equally disastrous. "I didn't hexpect to find a hunforgivin' spirit in you," he protests to James, and again, to the same antagonist: "Now you do yourself a hinjustice." Each of these examples represents a considerable refinement of the simple devices common to traditional orthographic rendering of cockney speech. Here the misplaced "h's" and other dialectal elements delight not merely as deviations comic in themselves but as speech actions made especially incongruous by the context in which they appear. The cockney habit of putting "h's" where they do not belong provides one sort of amusement; Burgess' habit of putting them on such elegant words as "unforgiving" and "injustice" provides amusement of a somewhat higher order. Shaw seems to use the misplaced "h" not merely where accuracy of transcription demands it, but where it will be most conspicuously incongruous or most vitally expressive. When, for instance, Burgess says to James: ". . . you certainly ain't as himpressive lookin' as usu'l," the "h" on "impressive" accents the telling epithet which embodies the real comic force of the line. The same principle operates in the line, ". . . hopinions becomes vurry serious things when people takes to hactin' on 'em as 'e does." Delightful even if rendered in Standard English, this vaguely paradoxical statement receives added force from the special emphasis placed on the two important words, "hopinions" and "hactin' " by the addition of the initial "h." The prefixing of this element, while adding explosive power to each word, also underscores the antithesis between the words, thus enhancing the effectiveness of the statement as a whole. That these examples represent deliberate artifice on Shaw's part, seems substantiated by a remark he makes in his essay on "English and American Dialects." "As to the interpolated "h," he writes, "my experience as a London vestryman has convinced me that it is often effective as a means of emphasis, and that the London language would be poorer without it."[11]

Shaw also manipulates other features of the dialect to serve the ends of comedy. Witness the following:

Yes, times 'as changed mor'n I could a believed. Five yorr [year] ago, no sensible man would a thought o' takin' up with your ideas. I hused to wonder you was let preach at all. Why, I know a clorgyman that 'as bin kep' hout of his job for yorrs by the Bishop of London, although the pore feller's not a bit more religious than you are. But to-day, if henyone was to offer to bet me a thousan' poun' that you'll end by bein' a bishop yourself, I shouldn't venture to take the bet. You and yore crew are gettin' hinfluential: I can see that. They'll 'ave to give you something someday, if it's only to stop yore mouth. You 'ad the right instinc' arter all, James: the line you took is the payin' line in the long run fur a man o' your sort.

The thought Burgess expresses here — the hardheaded, materialistic analysis of Morell's religious calling — makes up the comic essence of the passage. But the mode of utterance also contributes to the effect. The choice of words helps to make the speech a marvelous piece of debunking. The ministry becomes a "job" and

a "line," and its members make up a "crew." Morell himself —
the silver-tongued orator, darling of pulpit and platform — has
been "let preach," and it's a "bet" that he will someday be made
a bishop if it's only to "stop his mouth." Here the gruff heartiness of colloquial speech collides in comic incongruity with a
subject matter worthy of richer linguistic raiment.

In somewhat the same fashion, Burgess deflates "Morchbanks." "No, not ill. Only horror, horror, horror," the young
poet cries, with that exquisite agony he commands so well.
"What! Got the 'orrors, Mr. Morchbanks!" Burgess replies. "Oh,
that's bad, at your age. You must leave it off grajally." The joke
of course lies in Burgess' misconception of the meaning of "horror," but the corresponding corruption of the word itself reinforces the point.

Finally, we may notice one instance of a pun made possible by
the vicissitudes of cockney articulation. No fan of his illustrious
son-in-law, Burgess begs off when invited to attend one of James'
lectures, but quickly shifts ground when he learns that a member
of the all-powerful Works Committee is to be present. "Course I'll
come, James," he puts in hastily. "Ain' it always a pleasure to
'ear you."*

All of these instances seems to indicate that Shaw uses the
cockney dialect here not simply for realistic representation of
character, nor for its innate picturesqueness — though it serves
both these functions. Instead, he seems to go beyond these
effects to make this particular variety of low speech an instrument of comic power of a somewhat higher order. He uses the
misplaced "h" and other elements of dialect, not merely because
accuracy demands them, but for purposes of comic emphasis, or
because they result in incongruity, either with other words or
with the thought, or both. In short, Burgess' cockney dialect
seems to represent a conscious manipulation of language for
comic effect.

* Saxe, apparently overlooking this example, calls the following "play on
words": "a hill turn," (for "ill turn"), "hall very well," and "I ham," but
as the words thus formed have no significance in the context, they can
hardly be more than meaningless accidents, as indeed " 'ear" may also
be. (John Saxe, Phonetics, p. 47).

At the same time, it can hardly be said that the device contributes much, either to the characterization of Burgess or to the comic power of the play as a whole. Even the rendering of the dialect simply as a real mode of utterance intrinsically mirth-provoking, is scarcely more than fragmentary. Compared to the minutiae of other authors' painstaking transcriptions, and Shaw's own on other occasions, the efforts with Burgess remain little more than suggestions. He provides enough to distinguish the agent from other agents, to assign him to a class, and to make him more or less a figure of fun, but the full comic potentialities of the idiom remain for the most part untapped.* Moreover, even such pleasure as the language does afford remains tangential, at best, to powers more central in the work. Though a memorable figure — Auden has said that Shaw's "most lovable characters are rogues like Candida's father" — Burgess remains of minor interest while the spectator follows the working out of the love triangle.

Similarly, other uses of language remain severely attenuated. As already noted, Burgess sometimes attempts to mimic, with ludicrous results, his linguistic betters, but Shaw does not pursue the point and it adds little to the comic make-up of the character. This aspect of Burgess' speech habits does relate to materials given rather extensive development in the play, but not to any marked degree. As certain critics have noted, the conflict between Morell and Marchbanks often takes the form of a conflict of mere words, with Marchbanks spouting the airy formulas of neo-Platonism and Morell countering with the bromides of pulpit and public forum.[12] Burgess' taste for effective phrases might therefore be viewed as a variation on this central theme. His speech also serves to highlight this aspect of the central action on those isolated occasions when he unconsciously directs attention to the absurdity of their verbal posturings, as in his mangling of the meaning and sound of "horror."

But when all this has been said, the fact remains that Shaw had little interest on this occasion in full-scale exploitation of the comic potentialities of cockney dialect. That Burgess' mode of

---

* The fact that Burgess has risen to the ranks of the middle class accounts for the lack, of course. I do not mean to suggest that he should have been portrayed as more of a cockney, but only to measure the amount of comic language present in the play.

utterance contributes "summat," as he would say, to the play's overall comic power, seems sufficiently borne out by the evidence presented above. That its contribution remains minimal is apparent.

When Shaw next turned to cockney dialect, he went at his task a good deal more industriously. Felix Drinkwater, of *Captain Brassbound's Conversion* (1899), appears on the stage with a fool's costume of words comparable to the most ludicrous linguistic garb any comic agent ever donned. Burgess seems a mere sketch beside him, and the later dialect characters — though as richly endowed in other ways — scarcely rival him in comic mode of utterance.

Though similar in many ways, Drinkwater's speech differs markedly from Burgess' in the increased attention given to vulgarization of vowel sounds. Barely hinted at in the earlier character, this essential feature of the dialect colors practically every word Drinkwater utters. Qualitative deviations, as in "smawshing" for "smashing" and "kerrickter" for "character," vie for prominence with capricious lengthenings, as in "judeecial" and "cornduck." Such vowels as escape these operations undergo a drastic shortening — as in "nass" for "nurse" — or disappear altogether, as in "gavner" for "governor," "steblish" for "establish," and "spex" for "expects." Coupled with the various curiosities of consonant usage, these aberrations yield a marvel of strangeness seldom exceeded on the comic stage. Grouped together in such lines as "hoonawted we stend: deevawdid we fall," and "Wornt bawn in Hitly at all, lidy," these abominations easily arouse our primitive pleasure in the triumph of misrule.

* * *

In addition to standard articulatory distortions, Shaw stitches into the crazy quilt of Drinkwater's speech a pronounced idiosyncrasy of syntax, which consists in the reiteration, at the ends of sentences, of subject and verb, or, more often, of subject and auxiliary verb:

Ay sy nathink agin im: awm all fer lor mawseolf, *aw em.*

Walked acrost Harfricar with nathink but a little dawg, and wrowt abaht it in the Dily Mile, *she did.*

Waw, its spreadin civilawzytion, *it is.*

Sometimes, the reiteration takes a more elaborate form:

Deceased wawfe's sister: yuss, thets wot she is.
Hawce barrer and street pianner Hawtellian, lidy: thets wot e is.

Sometimes it occurs after both clauses of a compound sentence:
"Bin hattecked baw the Benny Seeras, *we ev,* an ed to rawd for it
pretty strite, too, *aw teoll yr.*

Though apparently indigenous to the dialect, (other Shaw
cockneys, especially Eliza, also use it) the device occurs with
sufficient frequency here to suggest a kind of compulsive tic. As
such, it shows some affinity with that element of the comic
which Bergson describes as "something mechanical encrusted on
the living." Ludicrous simply by dint of repetition like Tony
Lumpkin's addiction to the expletive "Ecod," the habit also
signalizes an important aspect of Drinkwater's character. The
constant victim of considerable abuse, not only from Brassbound
but from his fellow brigands as well, he is always at great pains to
achieve the sort of recognition he feels he deserves. We get the
most explicit revelation of his exaggerated opinion of himself in
his final speech, when he drops a none too subtle hint to his
temporarily leaderless colleagues, that he might be the man to
succeed the wavering Brassbound. "Brassbahnd ynt the ownly
kepn in the world," he announces. "Wot mikes a kepn is brines
and knollidge o lawf. It ynt thet thers naow sitch pusson: its thet
you dunno where to look fr im." As Shaw indicates in his stage
direction, "The implication that he is such a person is so intolerable that they [the men] receive it with a prolonged burst of
booing." In view of these facts about Drinkwater's posture before
the world, it may well be that his penchant for reiteration represents a feeble attempt to insure himself a hearing. Habitually
greeted with waves of indifference or howls of derision, he seems
to have hit upon this little trick of emphasis to extract from his
listeners the attention he regards as his due.

Such effects pale, however, beside the central joke embodied
in Drinkwater's use of the language. That joke consists of an antic

disparity between a nicety of sentiment and word choice, and the wrenched, warped, and willfully devious character of the sounds employed in their utterance. With significant regularity, the grotesqueries of Drinkwater's cockney vowels and consonants stand out in comic contrast to the thoughts they express or the words they form. Thus, in one of his first speeches to Rankin, he displays a refinement of feeling and phrase which has little in common with the vulgarisms of his articulation. "Lor bless yer, wawnt it you as converted me? Wot was aw wen aw cam eah but a pore lorst sinner? Dawnt aw ow y'a turn fer thet?"

The comic essence of these lines consists in the rather obvious insincerity of the sentiments they express. His styling himself a "pore lorst sinner," is so transparently hypocritical that we must laugh at its very blatancy. But one of the signs by which we infer this comic excess of feigned righteousness, is the patent incongruity between the lofty phrase and the lowly sounds with which the phrase is voiced. The vulgarity of the phonetic elements makes it abundantly clear that the phrase does not belong to this man's natural mode of expression. Other elements in the speech strengthen this impression. The lapse into one of the common vagaries of cockney syntax, in the phrase "you *as* converted me" and the colloquialism of the expression "ow y'a *turn* fer thet," join with the outlandish vowels and wayward consonants to emphasize the pretentious character of "Lor bless yer," and "pore lorst sinner."

If the comic contrast appeared only on this one occasion, it would warrant scant attention, but it shows itself again and again. It constitutes, in fact, the most salient feature of Drinkwater's speech and serves as a major device of comic characterization.

In some instances, the mawkishness of sound clashes with a studied elevation of feeling, actual word choice having little part in the structure: "Their mawnds kennot rawse to Christiennity lawk hahrs ken, gavner: thets ah it is." Here Drinkwater's fatuous claim to superiority over the "eathen," clashes absurdly with the marked inferiority of his mode of utterance. The grand manner of his constant references to Brassbound as "maw friend and commawnder Kepn Brarsbahnd of the schooner Thenksgivin" belongs to the same class of effects.

But more often, pretty turns of phrase like "pore lorst sinner," make up an essential part of the device. Constantly seeking to pass himself off as a Christian gentleman of considerable learning and refined sensibility, Drinkwater habitually adopts language patterns which he thinks will convey these qualities, only to be tripped up by his ever-present dialectal peculiarities. Asked why Brassbound is called Black Pakeetow, he frames his reply in the ordered structure of a scientific definition: "Waw, the bird in its netral stite bein green, an e evin bleck air, y'knaow—." Vaguely reminiscent of the First Gravedigger's lofty "your water is a sore decayer of your whoreson dead body," not to mention the chop-logic of innumerable other Shakespearean boobies, this variety of linguistic posturing is of ancient lineage.

When he is not affecting the schoolman's precision of state-ment, Drinkwater counterfeits angelic innocence and saintly humility by choosing appropriately devout terms. "Awm wanne of the missionary's good works," he tells Lady Cicely, "—'is first convert, a umble British seaman." When Sir Howard questions him about his police record, he is again ready with a polite phrase to whitewash his skullduggery. "Owny the aw sperrits of youth, y'lawdship. Worterleoo Rowd kice. Wot they calls Ooliganism." Asked the meaning of "Ooliganism," he is again equal to the occasion. "Nime giv huz pore thortless leds baw a gent on the Dily Chronicle," he answers. But perhaps the most richly comic example of Drinkwater's facility with the cant and euphemisms of the social worker and the churchman occurs in an early line to Rankin. Speaking of the fortunes of Brassbound's father, Rankin's former friend, he sighs: "Dear me! We cams hin with vennity, an we deepawts in dawkness. Down't we, gavner?"

On every possible occasion Drinkwater dons a rich mantle of sententiousness. But try as he may, he cannot conceal the true color of the workaday clothing beneath. In fact, the attempt is so grossly inept and the disguise so easily perceived, that the strat-agem produces simple delight in the fantastic rather than the punitive laughter sometimes evoked by such pretention and gran-diloquence. Drinkwater's speech habits amuse in somewhat the same fashion as the sight of a little girl parading in the cast-off finery of her mother.

But he delights not only because he dresses up in such ill-fitting finery, but also because the garments he chooses are themselves a bit silly looking. Last year's fashionable hat, perched precariously on the head of a child, arouses mirth not only because the child's head fails to fill it, but also because the hat itself, thus removed from the social setting which made it acceptable, now looks totally ridiculous. Drinkwater's "umble British seaman," "pore thortless lads," and other such outworn niceties are in somewhat the same case.

Some of these pretty locutions he has picked up from diligent reading of sensational and sentimental fiction, especially *Sweeny Todd, The Demon Barber of London,* and *The Skeleton Horseman.* Threatened with the deprivation of these treasures, he begs Lady Cicely's intercession, couching his plea, significantly enough, in the very terms these works have taught him to bandy: "Down't let em burn em, Lidy. They dassen't if you horder em not to. Yer dunno wot them books is to me. They took me aht of the sawdid reeyellities of the Worterleoo Rowd. They formed maw mawnd: they shaowed me sathink awgher than the squalor of a corster's lawf—." Redbrook's "Oh shut up, you fool," silences him at this point, else he might presumably have gone on to even loftier flights of eloquence.

Thus, with unflagging singleness of purpose, Drinkwater borrows fine words and phrases which his capricious cockney tongue can only render in the most absurdly distorted fashion. Whether solemnly murmuring the clichés of Christian comfort or sobbing out the formulas of pulp fiction bathos, he consistently arouses comic pleasure by the contrast of these tinsel terms with the hard realities of his cockney articulation.

Shaw has again proceeded quite deliberately, it would seem. His description of Drinkwater's speech suggests that he knows precisely what he is about; his "utterance," he says, is "affectedly pumped and hearty, — and naturally vulgar and nasal, . . . ready and fluent: nature, a Board School education, and some kerbstone practice having made him a bit of an orator."[13]

Drinkwater figures a good deal more prominently in the action of *Captain Brassbound's Conversion* than Burgess does in *Candida,* but he remains a secondary character nonetheless. Nor do his linguistic curiosities relate in any explicit fashion to the central action. Bentley points out that the major characters in the play "*are* the minor characters more closely examined and at a higher level of consciousness," and goes on to compare Drinkwater with Brassbound.[14] But the similarity does not appear to extend to their speech styles. On occasion, both tend to talk like characters in a stage melodrama, but Drinkwater employs the language of missionary tracts and Rankin's sermons more often than the bombast of *Sweeny Todd,* while Brassbound speaks quite regularly in the latter style, as will be seen in a later chapter.

Whether related to the central action or not, Drinkwater's peculiarities of utterance remain an important source of comic power in the play; their depth and extent make him one of the most outstanding exemplars of the comic in words in the entire Shaw canon.

Henry Straker of *Man and Superman* (1903), written some four years after *Captain Brassbound,* is also a cockney, but Shaw's handling of him differs importantly from his earlier methods with Burgess and Drinkwater; Straker might be thought of as the negative of the London type of which the earlier characters represent the positive image.

Introducing Straker, Shaw makes a point of telling us that he "does not at all affect the gentleman in his speech," and that observation signalizes the variation upon a theme which Shaw is to employ in delineating this character. Like Drinkwater, Straker is Board School educated, but unlike him has gone on to the Polytechnic. This experience with higher education, besides making him a paragon among automobile mechanics, has given him a natural turn for a more refined English, the like of which his earlier compatriots could only ineptly counterfeit. His speech thus contains a similar mixture of the street and the study, but his attitude toward this two-way linguistic pull differs radically from the stance adopted by Burgess and Drinkwater. If Candida's father and Brassbound's henchman consciously strive for elegance, and plummet ludicrously into cockney irregularity, Straker labors to *retain* his working-class diction but slips naturally into educated usage. The resulting incongruity greatly amuses John Tanner, whose observations upon it let the spectator in on the joke.

The device begins to work very shortly after Straker's first appearance, in Act II. Introducing his chauffeur to Octavius, Tanner mischievously calls him "Enry Straker," which prompts a good-natured but amusingly patronizing explanation from Straker to Octavius: "Pleased to meet you, sir. Mr. Tanner is gettin at you with is Enry Straker, you know. You call it Henery. But I don't mind, bless you." This wonderfully smug avowal of allegiance to the erroneous, Tanner cannot allow to pass; in commenting upon it he charges Straker with a sort of snobbery-in-reverse; defending himself to Octavius, he explains: "You think it's simply bad taste in me to chaff him, Tavy. But you're wrong. This man takes more trouble to drop his aitches than ever his father did to pick them up. It's a mark of caste to him. I have never met anybody more swollen with the pride of class than Enry is."

Given Tanner's penchant for overstatement, we might be inclined to fault him for unfairness here, but we are not asked simply to take his word for it; later in the play, Shaw allows us to catch Straker in the very attitude Tanner attributes to him here. Sent by Miss Violet to fetch young Hector Malone, Straker is piqued when Malone Sr., of whose identity Straker knows nothing, imposes himself upon him: "At the hotel they told me that your name is Ector Malone—," Straker protests, his vaunted efficiency having been called into question. "*H*ector Malone," the old gentleman corrects him. "Hector in your own country," says Straker, with all the righteous anger of a Public School grammarian. "Over here you're Ector: if you avn't noticed it before you soon will." A few lines later, accused by Malone of denseness for having failed to guess he was young Hector's father, Straker returns to the point, meticulously dropping his aitches as he frames his rejoinder: "When we've ad you as long to polish up as we've ad im [Malone Jr.], perhaps you'll begin to look a little bit up to is mark. At present you fall a long way short. You've got too many aitches, for one thing."

Just prior to this squabble, in introducing Hector Malone Sr., Shaw analyzes the attitudes of the two combatants and in so doing gives further evidence of his keen interest in dialect at this time and of the kind of amusement it afforded him:

One can only guess that the original material of [Malone's] speech was perhaps the surly Kerry brogue; but the degradation of speech that occurs in London, Glasgow, Dublin, and big cities generally has been at work on it so long that nobody but an arrant cockney would dream of calling it a brogue now; for its music is almost gone, though its surliness is still perceptible. Straker, as a very obvious cockney, inspires him with implacable contempt, as a stupid Englishman who cannot even speak his own language properly. Straker, on the other hand, regards the old gentleman's accent as a joke thoughtfully provided by Providence expressly for the amusement of the British race, and treats him normally with the indulgence due to an inferior and unlucky species . . . .

The incidents thus far noted show Straker displaying his pride of dialect, a class chauvinism which clings to the most minute particle of linguistic singularity with the tenacity of a state clinging to its hoariest and most sacrosanct institutions. But for all this insistence on minding his aitches, Straker elsewhere betrays what would today be called his upward social mobility by slipping easily into phrases of a decidedly non-cockney ambience, providing still further delight to the ever-watchful Tanner. When Tanner accuses Straker of "pride of class," in the speech already quoted, Straker gently rebukes him with "Easy, easy! A little moderation, Mr. Tanner," upon which Tanner immediately pounces with: "A little moderation, Tavy, you observe. You would tell me to draw it mild." Not long after, Straker uses a similarly cultivated expression and gets the same mocking response from Tanner:

TANNER: . . . if you can manage so as to be a good deal occupied with me, and leave Mr. Robinson a good deal occupied with Miss Whitefield, he will be deeply grateful to you.

STRAKER: Evidently.

TANNER: "Evidently!" Your grandfather would have simply winked.

Thus found out again, Straker seems to be trying to recover lost ground with his next line: "My grandfather would have touched his at," he says, and we are surely justified in supposing that he places special emphasis on that aitchless "at."

None of this takes up very much time in the play; as usual, Shaw's major comic effects are of a different kind. But such sporting with language as Shaw does indulge in here reveals his continuing interest in the comic possibilities of cockney dialect. At the risk of being a bit fanciful, one might speculate that the subject keeps intruding upon Shaw's consciousness as he labors at fashioning plays dealing primarily with other topics. The comedy of dialect keeps nagging at him, as it were, and he turns aside from his appointed rounds to give it temporary attention, only to go on shortly about his business. If this is true, then he finally exorcised the nagging imp only ten years later, with his most extensive treatment of dialect in *Pygmalion.*

Meanwhile, he continued to dally with it. *Man and Superman* itself has two other cockney characters, The Rowdy Social-Democrat and The Sulky Social-Democrat, members of Mendoza's band of highwaymen. Their speech is composed of the usual clump of linguistic wildflowers, but Shaw leaves the undergrowth just as he finds it; it is simply straightforward cockney, presented without the manipulation evident in the cases of Burgess, Drinkwater, and Straker.

In his next play, *John Bull's Other Island* (1904), Shaw pulls out several more stops and gives the play crashing chords of low speech nearly as numerous and prolonged as those in *Brassbound.* Never a man to be content with what was done last time, however, he improvises yet another new set of variations. Specifically, he adds Irish dialect to his repertoire and achieves some original effects with it, both in his handling of the brogue itself and in contrasting it with the cockney idiom.

In all of his more protracted treatments of low speech, Shaw reveals an interest in the comic possibilities of change and variety in an individual's speech habits; he tends to regard the dialect as a piece of equipment which can be donned or laid aside at will, or mixed with linguistic trappings of another order. We have seen this tendency operating with Burgess and Drinkwater, and in a somewhat different manner, with Straker. Similarly, the dialect characters in *John Bull's Other Island* are found changing in and out of their linquistic habiliments.

The first of these changes occurs in the opening scene of the play. Tom Broadbent, about to embark for Ireland on a real estate venture, is interviewing Tim Haffigan, an Irishman of his recent acquaintance, with a view to taking him along on the junket as a sort of liaison man with the natives. Haffigan's speech is as yeasty a concoction of the dialect as could be found outside the pages of Synge or O'Casey. "Top o the mornin," "Begorra," "Bedad," "More power to your elbow," "may your shadda never be less," and similar expressions adorn his every utterance. Shaw allows the spectator to savor and enjoy them for the length of some six pages before springing his surprise; at that point, Larry Doyle, Broadbent's partner and himself an expatriate Irishman, happens upon the scene, whereupon Haffigan's speech undergoes an abrupt and radical transformation, "decaying," as Shaw says, "into a common would-be genteel accent with an unexpected strain of Glasgow in it." After Haffigan, thoroughly discomfited, has made a hasty exit, Doyle explains everything to Broadbent, and to us. It seems that the "Typical" Irishman we have been smiling fondly over is no Irishman at all, but a native of Glasgow who has never been in Ireland in his life. When Broadbent protests that he spoke just like an Irishman, Doyle gives him an impassioned lecture on the true provenance of the dialect:

Like an Irishman! Man alive, dont you know that all this top-o-the-morning and broth-of-a-boy and more-power-to-your-elbow business is got up in England to fool you, like the Albert Hall concerts of Irish music? No Irishman ever talks like that in Ireland, or ever did, or ever will.

The joke is on Broadbent, and on us, and it is a more complicated joke than the rendering of Irish dialect usually involves. In arranging it, Shaw is exercising his usual habit of taking low speech and turning it inside out or standing it on its head or otherwise bending it about to suit his comic purposes.

This is not to say, however, that Doyle's view of the matter is to be taken as Shaw's own. Doyle almost certainly overstates the case; in so doing, he is giving vent to the deep distaste for all things Irish which he reveals throughout the play. At any rate, some such interpretation seems to be demanded by the full text, since in later scenes Shaw gives native Irish characters a similar brogue without any suggestion that it is merely affected. At the beginning of Act Two, in a scene that closely parallels the Haffigan scene at the beginning of Act One, he does have Father

Keegan affect a brogue in his conversation with the grasshopper, but he makes it clear that it is a style of speech which really exists among the peasants of Ireland. This is clearly stated in the stage direction, where Keegan is said to be "addressing the insect in a brogue which is the jocular assumption of a gentleman and not the natural speech of a peasant." The spectator in the theatre, lacking this information, is given a surprise after a few lines when Keegan drops the brogue to address Patsy Farrell, who has interrupted his bucolic colloquy. But Patsy himself has the brogue, and if it is an affectation for Keegan it is clearly natural speech for Patsy, as it is for other peasant characters who appear later. The truth of the matter would thus seem to be that the dialect, as usually represented on the stage, is in some measure, but not entirely, a fabrication of British imagination.

A third important dialect scene in the play involves another member of the Haffigan clan, Tim's Uncle Matthew, a genuine Irishman. In this scene the focus is not so much on Haffigan as upon his cockney interlocutor, Hodson, but it again involves a surprising shift of speech style. Hodson, Broadbent's valet, is introduced in the first scene of the play, and speaks there in a "standard" style, unmarked by regional peculiarity. He continues to express himself in that fashion until he is set upon by Haffigan, late in Act Three. Haffigan, an old bore on the subject of Ireland's sufferings at the hands of the English, attacks Hodson as a representative of his putative persecutors, calling him "sleek" and accusing him of having "an aisy time of it." At this affront, Hodson's national pride wells up in him and he immediately reverts to the cockney dialect, almost as though he were snatching the ancestral sword off the castle wall to do battle with the ancient enemy. "Suddenly dropping the well-spoken valet," as Shaw says, "and breaking out in his native cockney," he retorts: "Wots wrong with you, aold chep? Ez ennybody been doin ennything to you?" This sample of the genuine article is to be contrasted with such earlier speeches as his replies to Broadbent in the opening scene, where they are discussing the trip to Ireland: "I understand it's a very wet climate, sir. I'd better pack your india-rubber overalls;" or, "Is it a dangerous part you're going to, sir? Should I be expected to carry a revolver, sir?"

Having once abandoned the studied euphony of the Gentleman's Gentleman, he shows himself as fully the master of his linguistic birthright as Drinkwater himself. The set-to with Haffigan is a veritable feast of phonetic strangeness, with cockney and brogue vying for honors in the multilation of the language. The following sample is typical:

HODSON: . . . I'm jast sick of Awrland. Let it gow. Cat the caible. Mike it a present to Germany to keep the aowl Kyzer busy for a wawl; and give poor aowld England a chawnce: thets wot Oi sy.

MATTHEW: Take care we don't cut the cable ourselves some day, bad scran to you! An tell me dhis: have yanny Coercion Acs in England? Have yanny Removable magisthruts? Have you Dublin Castle to suppress every newspaper dhat takes the part o your own country?

HODSON: We can beyive ahreselves withaht sich things.

MATTHEW: Bedad youre right. It'd ony be waste o time to muzzle a sheep.

As usual, of course, the comic spine of the scene lies in what is said more than in how it is said; Shaw seldom contents himself with inviting laughter at dialect itself, after the manner of numberless vaudevillians. But the complete facility with both dialects exhibited here is no insignificant part of Shaw's artistry, and Hodson's sudden shift into the dialect is one of those *coups de theâtre* which make nonsense of the old charge that Shaw was merely a journalist masquerading as a dramatist. Such vignettes reveal him as a complete man of the theatre, willing and able, like most great playwrights, to take the proven, stock devices of the popular stage and join them to his higher purposes.

The cockney characters in Act II of *Major Barbara* (1905), though memorable in many respects, may be passed over rather hastily here, for on this occasion Shaw pays scant attention to the comic potentialities of the dialect. The natural vitality of the idiom affords its usual pleasure, of course, but it remains primarily a device of realistic characterization. On only two occasions does this feature of the language reach a pitch similar to that of the earlier plays. Snobby Price calls Peter Shirley a "jumped-up, jerked-off, orspittle-turned-out incurable of an ole workin man,"* and Rummy Mitchens calls Bill Walker a "flat-eared, pignosed potwalloper." For sheer ingenuity and crackling exuberance, these two sets of vulgar epithets nearly rival the most pungent of the exchanges between Falstaff and Hal. Unfortunately they remain rather isolated examples, though Snobby, Rummy and Bill all seem to display a good deal more saltiness in word choice than either Burgess or Drinkwater.

Snobby perhaps deserves additional notice because of certain similarities with Drinkwater. Like his predecessor, Snobby has mastered the style of his benefactors and can be quite handy with it when the occasion demands. "I could almost be glad of my past wickedness if I could believe that it would elp to keep hathers stright," he sanctimoniously confesses to Barbara. Elsewhere, he makes a similarly incongruous display of the language of self-righteousness, but nowhere with more telling effect than in his solemn declaration that he has "the peace that passeth hall hannerstennin."

Bill Walker, most prominent of this group of characters, provides a good deal of comic pleasure, but his style of speech has little to do with it, except in a rather roundabout fashion. His struggle to escape with honor the jesuitical subtleties of Barbara's campaign for his soul, constitutes the chief source of merriment, but the unyielding toughness of his manner of speaking perhaps contributes something to the humour of his predicament. Equipped only with the language of the barroom, he has a difficult time indeed dealing with the soft verbal persuasiveness of an "earl's grendorter." Thus, he longs "to be out o' the reach o' [Barbara's] tongue" and constantly complains about her talkativeness. His comic plight, which somewhat resembles the condition of a dog in a sweater, stems largely from his natural ferocity, and in so far as his mode of utterance reflects that quality, it may be said to contribute to the overall comic effect.

---

* Shaw seems to find the line particularly tangy himself; he repeats it almost verbatim in *The Shewing-up of Blanco Posnet.* Blanco has, "you all started in to be bad men or you wouldnt be in this jumped-up, jerked-off, hospital-turned-out camp that calls itself a town."

Yet Snobby, Rummy and Bill evoke little more in the way of strictly linguistic delight than the intrinsic eccentricity of cockney dialect naturally produces. As characters rendered ludicrous by virtue of distinctive habits of expression, they probably rank below Burgess and certainly below Drinkwater.

Shaw continues to depict dialect characters in the plays of the next few years. *Passion, Poison, and Petrifaction* (1905) has a cockney Landlord but he does not differ from other such minor characters already examined; Collins, of *Getting Married* (1908), seems to be of lower-class origins, though he has risen, but if Shaw intends him to be played with some measure of the dialect, he does not so indicate, either in stage directions or by phonetic spelling. Mrs. Farrell, of *Press Cuttings* (1909), is a compatriot of the Haffigans, but does not have Tim's chameleonic nature or a command of the dialect in any way distinguishable from Matthew's. The Orderly, in the same play, sometimes echoes Drinkwater in his ability to express subtleties of thought and feeling in crudities of language, but he is by and large a "straight" cockney, like his relatives in *Major Barbara*.

Indeed, all of the dialect characters encountered so far might be regarded as studies, made in preparation for the masterwork on the subject, that masterwork being *Pygmalion* (1913). To speak in such a fashion may be to slight such superb characters as Straker and Bill Walker, but it helps to show the continuity of Shaw's efforts with these materials. Certainly the two Doolittles are Shaw's greatest creations of this kind, and the play in which they appear is his most complete and most effective treatment of low speech generally and cockney dialect in particular. To notice that the Doolittles and *Pygmalion* have their antecedents in earlier works, some of them important, some of them trifles, is to catch a glimpse of Shaw's artistic *modus operandi*.

As all of this suggests, Eliza and Alfred display comic traits of usage basically similar to those exhibited by their less illustrious forbears. The same ludicrous distortions of the sounds of Standard English flavor their every syllable and these vulgarisms are again incongruously harnessed to a semi-refined vocabulary and syntax.

Alfred, in particular, provokes laughter by his frequent employment of a speech style all out of keeping with the lowliness of his vowels and consonants.* The neat rhetorical turn of his "I'm willing to tell you. I'm wanting to tell you. I'm waiting to tell you," unlooked for in the mouth of a "common dustman," easily arouses the amused admiration of Higgins and can hardly fail to delight the audience as well.

More often than not, his polished phrases collide not only with his phonetic distortions, but also with other elements of the vernacular, especially slang words and expressions, as in: "I can't carry the girl through the streets like a bloomin monkey, can I? I put it to you." Here the formal ring of "I put it to you," a phrase common to legal debate, sounds ludicrous beside the homely "bloomin monkey." In another speech, he strides imperiously through a nicely balanced parallelism, only to butt square against a barbarism of grammar: "Just one good spree for myself and the missus, giving pleasure to ourselves and employment to others, and satisfaction to you to think it's not been throwed away." In his "What am I, Governors both?" he takes the familiar cockney term of address "Governor," converts it to a very mannered plural, and uses it in that perennial of florid oratory, the rhetorical question.

The most pronounced and most delightful example of this tendency is Alfred's persistent sporting with the phrase "deserving poor," that indispensible shibboleth of the professionally charitable. Having decided that he belongs to the "*un*deserving poor," he frequently enlarges on the subject, pointing out the drawbacks of such a condition but admitting that it holds a certain attraction for him. "Undeserving poverty is my line," he avows. "Taking one station in society with another, it's — it's — well, it's the only one that has any ginger in it, to my taste."

In a similar fashion, he rather handily tosses about the phrase "middle-class morality," which he defines as "an excuse never to

* Shaw dispenses with phonetic spelling after Eliza's first speech, but he clearly intends both Doolittles to be spoken with the full complement of cockney sounds.

give [him] anything." When he comes into the Wannafeller Pre-digested Cheese annuity, he accuses Higgins of having "Tied me up and delivered me into the hands of middle-class morality." Deploring the fact that, as a man of means, he will now have to support his relatives and friends, he concludes: "I have to live for others and not for myself: that's middle-class morality."

These rhetorical flourishes, comic by contrast with the vulgarisms of diction which house them, seem to be part and parcel of the comic essence of Doolittle's character, rather than mere laughter-provoking devices gratuitously superimposed. For Doolittle, as he himself explicitly asserts on at least three separate occasions, is a "thinking man." He substantiates this claim to a certain refinement of intellectual perception by the quality of thinking he reveals in his various exchanges with Higgins and Pickering. Witness his shrewd analysis of his relations with his current "companion": "I'm willing [to marry her]. It's me that suffers by it. I've no hold on her. I got to buy her clothes something sinful. I'm a slave to that woman, Governor, just because I'm not her lawful husband. And she knows it too. Catch her marrying me!" Higgins also lends authority to the claim by avowing that with three-months' speech training behind him, Doolittle "could choose between a seat in the Cabinet and a popular pulpit in Wales."

This intellectual agility of Doolittle's, so amply evidenced in the play, seems to form the very core of his comic being. The juxtaposition of his better-than-average, if not superior, intellectual qualifications, with his questionable moral qualifications – as evidenced in his laziness, fondness for drink, etc., – produces a richly comic portrait. In fact, it is precisely this imbalance of natural proclivities which generates his comic dilemma; his irrepressible cleverness trips him up first by denying him a place in the ranks of the "deserving poor," and finally by bringing about that most dreaded calamity, his elevation to the middle class.

If this analysis of Doolittle's character and situation is correct, then his habits of speech may be seen to have an organic relationship with them. Just as the mental and moral aspects of his character jostle each other in comic incongruity, so do the stylistic and phonetic components of his speech; vulgarity of speech-sound parallels vulgarity of taste, while refinement of word-choice and arrangement parallels refinement of thought. Some such close connection between style of speaking and style of living seems substantiated, moreover, by a particularly significant revelation Doolittle makes to Higgins shortly after his first appearance. "Ive heard all the preachers and all the prime ministers — for I'm a thinking man and game for politics or religion or social reform same as all the other amusements—. . . ." The speech not only gives further evidence of his ability to function on the higher planes of thought, but also reveals the source of his turn for oratorical niceties of expression.

Though far less frequently and to a different end, Eliza's speech also embodies a ludicrous disparity of rank between word and sound. In her first scene, suddenly enriched by the coins Higgins has thrown at her feet, she decides to ride home in the taxi Freddy has secured for his already departed mother and sister. Anxious to conceal her lowly address from Freddy, she grandly announces to the cabman that she wishes to go to Buckingham Palace, but the subterfuge fails ignominiously when the words come out "Bucknam Pellis." The same sort of joke occurs again when she reaches her destination. Attempting to crush the taxi driver with a lofty rebuke for his familiarity, she can only come up with "Impidence."

Such minutiae as these, though obviously productive of at least a smile, might at first glance seem hardly worth noticing. But with these two deft strokes of his smallest brush, Shaw adds important detail to the canvas of his action. With consummate economy, both utterances show Eliza trying to pass herself off as a lady, and failing miserably because of her inescapable cockney articulation. In short, they prefigure the central action of the play.

Other features of Eliza's speech also arouse delight. That piercing cry of "Ah-ah-ah-ow-ow-ow," which Shaw has her use repeatedly, now to convey distress, now delight, incites amusement by virtue of its unmitigated ugliness; the sound seems to epitomize the complete animal abandon of cockney phonetics.

Eliza's lusty colloquialisms, her street-corner epithets and expletives also serve to make her speech a banquet of comic expressiveness. "You ought to be stuffed with nails," she tells

Higgins, a barb beside which the feeble "Impidence," mentioned above, seems inadequate indeed. When she knowingly whispers to Higgins that he must have emptied his pockets at her feet because he "had a drop in," the expression makes even moderate drinking sound so wonderfully frivolous as to be totally incongruous for the rigourously disciplined phonetician. Elsewhere, such tangy turns of phrase as "come off it," "ain't no call," and "off his chump" add to the general gusto of her untutored speech.

These characteristics Eliza's speech has in common with that of the other cockneys already considered. The intrinsic vitality of the dialect, the curiosities of sound and expression and the more or less frequent clash of vulgarized vocalization with elegant words, combine to lend comic force to Eliza's utterance in much the same way that they make Burgess, Snobby Price, Drinkwater and the rest a delight to hear.

* * *

But Eliza differs from her predecessors in two important particulars. Alone among them, Eliza's speech changes completely, and the process of that change makes possible a comic use of language all but denied to Shaw in his handling of the earlier characters. In accomplishing it, Shaw fully articulates a device he had experimented with only briefly and tentatively in allowing Straker and Hodson to shift about from low to high in phonetics and vocabulary. Compared with the handling of Drinkwater, Burgess, and others — as well as Eliza herself in earlier scenes — the new method amounts to a nearly complete reversal. Where the language of Drinkwater and his like aroused mirth by the collision of cockney enunciation with a florid vocabulary, Eliza's language, in one crucial scene, generates comic pleasure by the collision of her cockney vocabulary with the exquisitely sonorous vowels and sharply differentiated consonants Higgins taught her.

The scene occurs at the opening of Act Two. Higgins has decided to give his Galatea a trial run and has accordingly invited her to one of his mother's at-homes. Shaw prepares the audience for the ensuing debacle by having Higgins confide to his mother, before Eliza's arrival, that he has "got her pronunciation all right, but you have to consider not only how a girl pronounces but what she pronounces." Higgins also reveals that he has attempted to control "what she pronounces" by restricting her to two topics of conversation: "the weather and everybody's health," but despite his assurance that "that will be safe," the latter topic proves a disastrously unwise choice.

Eliza arrives and the merriment Shaw has so carefully contrived quickly follows, though not until the audience has first been led off on a false scent. As if to heighten the unexpectedness of what follows, Shaw first has Eliza's choice of expression move in a direction precisely opposite to the comic descent into vulgarity it is soon to make. "Will it rain, do you think?" Mrs. Higgins asks "conversationally." Recognizing her cue, the well-coached Eliza immediately volunteers: "The shallow depression in the west of these islands is likely to move slowly in an easterly direction. There are no indications of any great change in the barometrical situation." Hilarious in its own right, this impossibly stilted report is Eliza's first and last successful attempt at a decorous choice of phrase. Freddy finds the speech "awfully funny," even "Killing," and as though giving it up as a bad job in the face of his reaction, Eliza switches into more comfortable linguistic garb.

From this point on, her dulcet tones bump along on the backs of her vulgar words like a bishop on a runaway jackass. When Mrs. Eynsford Hill innocently turns the talk to influenza, Eliza easily recognizes the second of her "safe" topics and so joins in, presumably with every confidence that she is pleasing her watchful tutor. "My aunt died of influenza: so they said. But it's my belief they done the old woman in," she begins. Pressed for further details, she continues: "Y-e-e-e-es, Lord love you! Why should she die of influenza? She come through diptheria right enough the year before. I saw her with my own eyes. Fairly blue with it, she was. They all thought she was dead; but my father he kept ladling gin down her throat til she came to so sudden that she bit the bowl off the spoon." She goes on in the same style for the remainder of the short sequence, reaching a pinnacle of incongruity with the exit line: "Not bloody likely," which she intones, according to Shaw, "with perfectly elegant diction."

The events Eliza describes here, and the language in which she describes them, guarantee the scene a superlative comic effect in

themselves. Voiced in the polite atmosphere of a fashionable
at-home, her lurid narrative produces somewhat the same reaction
as might a pair of bare feet at a royal wedding. But the fact that
she relates this tale of tenement intrigue with the flawless
euphoniousness of a classical actor declaiming Shakespeare, surely
adds to the comic power of the scene. The ingenuity Shaw
displays on this occasion marks the apogee of his experiments
with the comic potentialities of low speech, and helps to make
Eliza one of the most entertaining dialect characters in the whole
of dramatic literature.

Eliza also differs from her fellow cockneys in another
important respect. Here, for the first and only time, Shaw uses
comic speech as a necessary condition of the central action of his
play. The speech of the other low comic agents adds to the
general merriment of the plays in which they appear in a strictly
tangential fashion. With the exception of possible oblique rela-
tionships, as already noted, their mode of utterance has nothing
to do with the basic antecedent-consequence scheme which
unifies the plays. Not so Eliza. Take away Drinkwater's cockney
speech and you will still have *Captain Brassbound's Conversion,*
fundamentally intact. Take away Eliza's and you will have a
basically different play. Eliza's speech sets in motion the plot-
character-thought complex which constitutes the play's very
essence.

But it does more than set it in motion. Shaw does not use the
confrontation of a cockney flower-girl and a zealous phonetician
merely as a framework for a retelling of the Pygmalion-Galatea
story. To be sure, once Higgins and Eliza have made their pact
and the lessons have begun, we become interested, no doubt
primarily interested, in dramatic questions stemming from the
familiar male teacher-female pupil situation: We wonder, that is,
whether Eliza will change in appearance and deportment as well
as manner of speech, whether Higgins will feel attracted to her
and she to him, whether she will attract and perhaps prefer other
admirers, and so on. We become interested, in short, in questions
which have nothing to do with the fact that the pupil is a
cockney and the master a phonetician; we follow with expecta-
tion the interaction of an unmarried, highly desirable *male*
teacher and an unmarried, potentially very desirable *female* pupil.

For all the difference it would make in the way we react to this dramatically fertile situation, Higgins could just as well be an Elizabethan courtier teaching table manners to a tavern wench.

Despite the fact that this Pygmalion-Galatea "romance" probably contains the bulk of the play's interest, the fact that this particular Pygmalion is a speech teacher and his Galatea a cockney badly in need of his ministrations, is not a matter of complete indifference. To a significant degree, the play is *about* speech in the same way and at the same time that it is about a certain male-female conflict. One of the dramatic questions which claims our attention as we follow the play is whether or not Higgins, by radically transforming Eliza's speech, will succeed in his scheme to "pass [her] off as a duchess at an ambassador's garden party." Aware of this plan, we view the various stages with emotionalized anticipation — hoping that it will succeed and fearing that it will not — after the usual manner of following a fictional intrigue.

But the speech correction-garden party story provides pleasure not only as an intrigue. The fact that it is speech alone* which is to make the difference between a flower girl and a duchess endows this action line with a fine satiric thrust at the basic artificiality of social ranking. The confrontation of correctionist and "patient" also provides a dramatically probable occasion on which Shaw can have his spokesman Higgins make other satiric comments on the place of speech in British society and on the deplorable lack of suitable training in the phonetics of the English language. Thus, on one occasion we hear him say:

This is an age of upstarts. Men begin in Kentish Town with £80 a year, and end in Park Lane with a hundred thousand. They want to drop Kentish Town; but they give themselves away every time they open their mouths.

And on another, to Eliza:

A woman who utters such depressing and disgusting sounds has no right to be anywhere — no right to live. Remember that you are a human being with a soul and the divine gift of articulate speech: that your native language is the language of Shakespeare and Milton and The Bible; and don't sit there crooning like a bilious pigeon.

* Not quite, of course; Higgins also instructs her in grooming, dress and manners but it is speech which is held to be the essential factor.

Such lines as these, together with the comic success-through-phonetics intrigue which prompts them, show the organic position of Eliza's speech in the structure of the play. In point of dramatic interest, these materials probably rank second to the Eliza-Higgins character clash,* but they far exceed the importance of cockney speech in Shaw's earlier plays.

Shaw uses the cockney idiom and additional varieties of low speech in other ways, but the figures treated here are the major ones and the comic characteristics of their speech seem amply representative. As I have tried to show, the device is of secondary importance compared to other techniques of Shavian comic dramaturgy, both from the standpoint of frequency of employment and contribution to the total comic effect of the plays in which it appears. Nevertheless, Shaw's manipulation of the language of the unlettered deserves attention in any complete assessment of the resources of his art. Though *Candida, Captain Brassbound's Conversion, Major Barbara* and *Pygmalion* owe the bulk of their power to other ingredients, the verbal motley of the cockney characters in these and other plays must claim a worthy share of the credit.

---

* Predictably, Shaw is on record with the opposite opinion. In a preface to the Penguin edition of the play, having pointed to the wide popularity of *Pygmalion,* he wrote: "[The play] is so intensely and deliberately didactic and its subject [phonetics] is esteemed so dry, that I delight in throwing it at the heads of the wiseacres who repeat the parrot cry that art should never be didactic. It goes to prove my contention that great art can never be anything else."

The play proves, of course, nothing of the sort. A theatre man of Shaw's acuity can hardly have been unaware of the great popular appeal of the Pygmalion-Galatea situation; he uses it deliberately and with great skill and if he manages to teach something about phonetics in the process, the fact remains that his play contains a great deal more than a lesson on that "dry subject." Employing his usual propagandistic tactic, the outrageous statement, Shaw misrepresents his own play but effectively renews his appeal for serious (equal "didactic") drama. *Pygmalion* is a didactic play on the subject of phonetics in approximately the same degree that *Othello* is a didactic play on the subject of miscegenation.

CHAPTER IV

Linguistic Satire

The humor in the speech of Shaw's cockney characters stems primarily from peculiarities of sound and word formation. Where word choice and arrangement figure in the effect, they do so by virtue of comic contrast with these oddities of sound. Elsewhere, Shaw uses vocabulary and syntax to achieve comic effects which have little or nothing to do with sound.

Whenever custom or conscious design formalizes language into more or less distinct and easily recognizable patterns, the resultant "styles" tend to be exceedingly vulnerable to mockery and ridicule. Like any other facet of human activity which veers off from the norm, like any other aspect of existence which becomes rigid and standardized, special vocabularies and coterie syntaxes provide the discerning humorist with ready material for the exercise of his art.

Playwrights have found such materials especially tantalizing. Shakespeare's Holofernes travesties the schoolmaster's jargon; Molière pokes fun at medical and legal gabble with Monsieur Fleurant of *Le Malade Imaginaire* and the notary of *L'École des Femmes*; Jonson ridicules the rhetoric of forum and pulpit with Adam Overdo and Zeal-of-the-Land Busy in *Bartholomew Fair*. And these represent but a fraction of the examples to be found in the pages of these comic masters.

When not burlesquing the technical language of pulpit, bar, and bedside, comic dramatists have mocked the stately rhythms and exotic vocabularies of their fellow literary artists. In the Pyramus and Thisby episode of *A Midsummer Night's Dream* Shakespeare parodies his own matchless diction. Buckingham's *Rehearsal*, Fielding's *Tom Thumb* and a host of less celebrated plays carry the tradition of literary satire forward to modern take-offs on O'Neill, Williams, Eliot, and others.

* * *

Linguistic satire of this type is usually accomplished by one or the other − or a combination − of two basic methods, each of which perhaps warrants some preliminary comment. In one, the parodist isolates those elements of his subject's style which individualize it; i.e., he discovers his victim's habits. In composing his caricature, he then simply exaggerates these features, adding outrageously to the frequency of their employment. Does Hemingway favor short, spare declaratives comprised chiefly of monosyllables? To travesty his style, one need only pile up such constructions to the near total exclusion of all other possibilities. The result is rigidity where one has a right to expect variety, and that, as Bergson and others have shown, is comic. The point of such a procedure is that the writer being burlesqued approaches absurdity in proportion as he favors inordinately this or that stylistic maneuver.

The point of the second method is somewhat more subtle, though it too sets up as the object of laughter a tendency toward inflexibility. Our sense of the natural and proper in linguistic matters allows for the formulation of distinctive patterns to suit distinctive ends. We permit the highly specialized in style where the most efficient communication of highly specialized information, or the achievement of highly specialized effects, seems to justify it. The poet is thus given leave to tell of his anguish in the unique fashion he has devised for that purpose, but the policeman on the corner had better not use the same instrument to direct us to the automat.

Aware of these facts, the parodist can evoke laughter at language by taking a special style and using it for a purpose other than the one for which it was intended. In so doing, he implies that the original writer, or group of writers, has in some degree been guilty of the same procedure; the familiar lampoons of the language of Sociology and Psychology are of this type; the allegation there is that much of the professional terminology is not really required by the phenomena being described, and that in using it the writer has failed to make a salutary adjustment of language to subject.

Shaw uses these methods, and variations upon them, to ridicule a variety of styles, in a number of both major and minor plays. Since the minor plays offer the clearest examples, it may be helpful to look first at them.

Shaw wrote *The Admirable Bashville or Constancy Unrewarded* in one week. Piqued by reports of several unauthorized American dramatizations of his 1881 novel about pugilism, *Cashel Byron's Profession*, he quickly dashed off his own stage version, paid to have it performed, and thus secured protection from further pirating, under Britain's copyright laws. Written in blank verse, because "it is so childishly easy . . . that . . . I was enabled to do within the week what would have cost me a month in prose,"[1] *Bashville* exploits the venerable burlesque device of contrasting elevated language with a homely subject. The verbal finery of Elizabethan verse drama clashes absurdly with the mock-heroic story of a prizefighter in love. Examples appear on virtually every page of the short play, but the following is perhaps one of the more graphic:

Dread monarch: this is called the upper cut,
And this a hook-hit of mine own invention.
The hollow region where I plant this blow
Is called the mark. My left, you will observe,
I chiefly use for long shots: with my right
Aiming beside the angle of the jaw
And landing with a certain delicate screw
I without violence knock my foeman out.
Mark how he falls forward upon his face!
The rules allow ten seconds to get up;
And as the man is still quite silly, I
Might safely finish him; but my respect
For your most gracious majesty's desire
To see some further triumphs of the science
Of self-defence postpones awhile his doom.

Elsewhere Shaw mocks more specific aspects of the idiom of poetic drama. With such phrases as "barely the bet was booked," and "perfidious peer," he travesties not only the device of alliteration but nicety of word choice and syntax as well. In lines like " ... patterns ... that lie, antimacassarly, asprent thy drawing-room," he ridicules the poet's fondness for the unusual in both vocabulary and grammar, while with "bruiséd grass," and "cakéd mud," he burlesques yet another common feature of the blank verse line.

But the numerous plagiarisms scattered throughout the play probably provide more fun than any of these devices. "He will not come again," the heroine sighs. "A consummation devoutly to be wished by any lady," her cousin answers. Lamenting the fact that he was born the son of an actress, the hero complains:

My earliest lesson was the player's speech
In Hamlet; and to this day I express myself
More like a mobled queen than like a man
Of flesh and blood. Well may your cousin sneer!
What's Hecuba to him or he to Hecuba?

Dipping still further into *Hamlet*, Shaw has his prizefighter begin an important match with the philosophical observation, "There's a divinity that shapes our ends, Rough hew them how he will. Give me the gloves."

The slight distortion of the borrowed line, evidenced in this last example, appears in several other places as well. Speaking of his "wretched mother," whom he intensely dislikes, Cashel prays: "Oh God, let me be natural a moment!" Later, leaving *Hamlet* for *As You Like It*, he laments the unhappy outcome of a fight with, "My training wasted and my blows unpaid. Sans stakes, sans victory, sans everything I had hoped to win."

Not to be outdone, his loved one follows almost immediately with "Oh, tiger's heart wrapped in a young man's hide ...."

Thus, in a variety of ways, Shaw directs attention to the essential artificiality of the language of poetic drama. An instrument deliberately fabricated for the expression of those intense emotions which in life remain unverbalized, blank verse naturally becomes ridiculous when applied to those mundane activities to which a less contrived style would clearly be better suited. By its failure to serve the needs of everyday living, the poetic idiom stands revealed in all its formality, and becomes comic in consequence. As one critic has it, "In forcing a stately and archaic verse to accommodate a modern and unrewarding theme, Shaw was making exactly the same joke as Fielding had made in describing a vulgar brawl in language suited to an Homeric combat. The vehicle is too fine for the passenger, the words too big for the sentiment."[2]

In *The Dark Lady of the Sonnets*, another *pièce d'occasion*, Shaw makes further sport of poetic diction. Though less a full-scale travesty than *Bashville*, *The Dark Lady* also glistens with familiar Shakespearean lines and phrases. This time Shaw enriches the joke by depicting Shakespeare himself copying down the felicitous turns of phrase as they tumble quite ingenuously from the mouths of various people he encounters on a midnight assignation with his dark lady. Much of the fun of the play thus resides in the spectacle of the greatest of English dramatic poets borrowing his finest figures from the casual conversation of contemporaries, but the very presence of these poetic beauties in such settings also represents a telling incongruity and emphasizes their artificiality. Thus, when The Beefeater, in the fourth line of the play, says: "Angels and ministers of grace defend us!" the ejaculation surely prompts a laugh even before the unidentified man with whom he shares the stage begs leave to set the words down in writing, because he has a "very poor and unhappy brain for remembrance." From this point forward, to be sure, the identity of The Man doubtless remains a mystery only to the totally unlettered, and the two jokes tend to operate as one, but their separability remains no less actual.

As in the earlier play, Shaw borrows almost exclusively from *Hamlet*, but though nearly identical in origin, the stolen lines vary in the use made of them. "I shall not return too suddenly unless my sergeant comes prowling round." says The Beefeater. "Tis a fell sergeant, sir: strict in his arrest." Here the theft permits word-play, involving the use of "Sergeant" in both its literal and figurative sense. Another time, a celebrated phrase suffers an ignominious down-grading of reference: "damned spot" becomes a smear of cosmetic in place of the blood of an annointed king.

But more often, Shaw simply tucks the purloined word or words into the conversation without special pointing, inviting laughter at the spectacle of a Pegasus forced to pull a plow. When The Man declares all women false, The Beefeater demurs tolerantly: "You judge too much by the Court, sir. There, indeed, you may say of frailty that its name is woman." Similarly, when The Man laments the fact that "We call one another names when we are offended, as children do," his philosophic friend replies: "Ay, sir: words, words, words. Mere wind, sir. We fill our bellies with the east wind, sir, as the Scripture hath it. You cannot feed capons so."

Shaw indulged this particular fancy on only one other occasion, in a short skit written for the Malvern Marionette Theatre, entitled *Shakes Versus Shav* (1949). In five pages of knockabout farce, it depicts a debate between Shaw and Shakespeare on the subject of their relative claims to immortality. Like *Bashville* and *Dark Lady*, it was composed with *The Complete Works of Shakespeare* open on the writing table. We hear " . . . damned be he that proves the smaller boy," and "There is more fun in heaven and earth, sweet William, Than is dreamt of in your philosophy," and "Tomorrow and tomorrow and tomorrow we puppets shall replay our scene," together with more oblique references to the Shakespearean manner, such as "Laughest thou at thyself?" and "Pullst thou my leg?"

The result of such manipulations is a triumph of mismatching, with Shakespeare taking a hazing in the process. As Shaw, the tireless foe of bardolators, fully realizes, the bard can afford it; in his Foreward to *Cymbeline Refinished*, Shaw remarks that "Shakespeare will survive any possible extremity of caricature."[3]

These three short pieces are Shaw on holiday. The major plays contain no fooling precisely of this sort. But a number of them do contain something like it. On a great many occasions Shaw depicts characters who have borrowed a style of speech, not so much from a single well-known author as from a whole genre of writing. Sergius, of *Arms and the Man* (1894), is the earliest example.

Arms and the Man represents a full-scale Shavian assault on the bastions of romanticism. The comic import of the play resides in the contrast between the storybook conceptions of love and war exhibited by Sergius and Raina, and Bluntschli's realistic, common-sense appraisals of these same avocations. This much critics have been quick to recognize, but the place occupied by language in the rendering of the comic action seems to have gone altogether unnoticed. It warrants some attention.

An early commentator on the play described Sergius as a man possessed of "a super-Byronic blatancy of soul"[4] and Bluntschli, recalling the famous cavalry charge, says Sergius conducted himself "like an operatic tenor." Both phrases succinctly describe this arch-romantic who, as Raina reveals, owes his inflated "heroic ideas" to a fondness for reading Byron and Pushkin, a fondness which she shares with her dashing fiancé.* Shaw characterizes Sergius as a man of this stamp by the attitudes he has him voice and the actions he has him perform. But he does not stop there. Sergius not only behaves like the hero of a romantic novel – he talks like one. He not only leads a foolhardy cavalry charge with mustachios bristling and sabre at the ready, he not only invests his loved one with attributes of perfection never attained by mortal woman, he not only challenges Bluntschli to a duel at dawn – he also brandishes a style of speech as absurdly grandiose as any of these attitudes and actions.

At the most elementary level, Sergius' style takes on a heroic cast appropriate to his heroic temperament, by virtue of certain elements of vocabulary which figure in it. He speaks often of love "trifled with" and honor "betrayed," employing two verbs so closely associated with romantic fiction that they have all but lost their usefulness in other contexts. Had Shaw given Sergius no more than this, he would have done much to mark him as fair game for ridicule. But he gives him a good deal more. "Damnation! Oh, Damnation!" Sergius cries on one occasion. And on

---

* As might be expected, given their similarity of temperament, Raina's speech exhibits roughly the same characteristics as Sergius', though her style remains closer to normal. Sergius being the greater buffoon of the two, his mode of utterance is proportionately more eccentric. Moreover, Sergius remains largely unregenerate, while Raina drops her pose, and her grandiloquence, when "found out" by Bluntschli.

another: "False! Monstrous!" And again: "Devil! Devil!" Like "trifle" and "betray" such oaths and imprecations clearly stamp their user as a man who has abandoned the speech of the real world to adopt instead the purple prose of the literature of chivalry.

That Shaw is here consciously employing such words and phrases for satiric purpose seems indicated by a statement he makes in the preface to *Overruled*. Inveighing against the "plays of the nineteenth-century Paris school," he catalogues the stock ingredients of such plays as follows: " . . . the convention that a man should fight a duel or come to fisticuffs with his wife's lover if she has one, . . . the convention that he should strangle her like Othello, or turn her out of the house and never see her or allow her to see her children again, . . . the convention that she should never be spoken to again by any decent person and should finally drown herself, . . . the convention that persons involved in scenes of recrimination or confession by these conventions *should call each other certain abusive names and describe their conduct as guilty and frail and so on . . . .*"[5]

Other features of Sergius' mode of utterance add to its novelistic flavor. Such pseudo-poetic locutions as "You lie," "I dare marry you," "You shall wait my pleasure," and "I brook no rivals," add their trumpet notes to swollen phrases like "A paltry taunt," "A hollow sham," and "huge imposture of a world." The knightly sobriquets Sergius so often substitutes for Bluntschli's commonplace name further reveal his penchant for the grand: he addresses him as "noble Switzer," "Switzer," and "My Professional."

His turn for the literary also appears in the fondness he shows for essentially artificial stylistic patterns. "If these hands ever touch you again," he tells Louka, "they shall touch my affianced bride," a line which echoes his earlier announcement to the effect that "This hand is more accustomed to the sword than to the pen." Both speeches smack of self-conscious artifice and indicate how fully Sergius has absorbed the hot-house sententiousness of the fictional stalwarts after whom he patterns his conduct.

Elsewhere, he embarks on verbal flights even further removed from the simple prose of workaday parlance. In the following speech, anaphora joins the rhetorical interrogative to produce a singularly elevated linguistic manner:

I am surprised at myself, Louka. What would Sergius, the hero of Slivnitza, say if he saw me now? What would Sergius, the Apostle of the higher love, say if he saw me now? What would the half-dozen Sergiuses who keep popping in and out of this handsome figure of mine say if they caught us here?

The elevated tone exhibited here occurs also in a similar passage, on a similar subject; further indulging in public introspection, he asks:

Which of the six is the real man? That's the question that torments me. One of them is a hero, another a buffoon, another a humbug, another perhaps a bit of a blackguard, and one, at least, is a coward: jealous, like all cowards.

This venerable oratorical device of framing queries which require no answers, claims Sergius' patronage on at least two other occasions as well. "Shall I kill myself like a man, or live and pretend to laugh at myself?" he asks. And again, "Are fresh abysses opening?"

The taste for balance and parallelism evidenced here in the repetition of "What would Sergius say . . . " and "another . . . another," also shows itself in other lines. "If you are away five minutes, it will seem five hours," he tells Raina prettily. Elsewhere, adding hackneyed hyperbole to his other gaudy verbalisms, he describes Raina as "a woman as high above you as heaven is above earth." The careful matching of clauses in "How is Raina, and where is Raina?" reflects a similar affectation.

But he seems to enjoy neat antitheses even more than these balanced pairs. Among the more clear-cut examples are:

She! Whose worst thoughts are higher than your best ones.

This is either the finest heroism or the most crawling baseness.

I won the battle the wrong way when our worthy Russian generals were losing it the right way.

Soldiering, my dear madam, is the coward's art of attacking mercilessly when you are strong, and keeping out of harm's way when you are weak.

In addition to these tropes and figures, Sergius' speech also contains other ornamental features. On occasion, he breaks into metaphor, as in:

Swiss civilization nursetending Bulgarian Barbarism, eh?

We were two children in the hands of that consummate soldier.

Madam; it was the cradle and the grave of my military reputation.

That shows that you are an abominable little clod of common clay.

At least once, he adopts the device of metonomy, to describe "real men" as "men of heart, blood, and honor." And at least once also his speech becomes quite alliterative; in the line, "The glimpses I have had of the seamy side of life during the last few months have made me cynical," the soft "s" sounds reinforce the exaggerated delicacy of the sentiment he voices.

Though scarcely noteworthy if considered individually, these several linguistic elements combine to produce a style of speech which contributes substantially to the comic characterization of the agent who displays them. A man who talks like the hero of a stage melodrama or a romantic novel naturally invites ridicule, and the habits of speech noted above make Sergius just such a man. His persistent substitution of the clichés of rhetorical and poetic contrivance, for the simpler words and patterns of ordinary prose discourse, constitutes a deviation from the linguistic norm established by other characters in the play and is laughable in consequence. Just as he adopts attitudes, makes decisions and performs actions which Shaw represents as comic departures from the happy mean, he also chooses words and phrases equally eccentric in character.

A comparison of his handling of the language with Bluntschli's way of using words, makes this abundantly clear. While Sergius strives everywhere for the attainment of the elevated, Bluntschli, not surprisingly, remains firmly rooted in the commonplace. Perhaps the simplest indication of this difference is the fact that Bluntschli uses contractions on virtually every possible occasion, while Sergius, with rare exceptions, pointedly eschews them.

But the differentiation goes deeper than this. Shaw seasons Bluntschli's speech with a liberal sprinkling of colloquialism of a type totally absent from Sergius' polished prose. Such everyday expressions as "nearly burst with laughter," "as white as a sheet," "a narrow shave," "by fits and starts," "cut us to bits," "got wind of," "in cold blood," and "live happily ever after," — to name only a few — tag Bluntschli's speech with a quality of spontaneity which contrasts sharply with the studied floridity of his antagonist's mode of utterance.

Similarly, the syntactical configurations of Bluntschli's oral style differ markedly from the more or less formal arrangements Sergius regularly employs. Disdaining such elaborate rhetorical strategies as antithesis and parallel, Bluntschli couches his thoughts in clusters of short, simple sentences stripped down to the barest essentials, as in the following:

I musn't judge her. I once listened myself outside a tent when there was a mutiny brewing. It's all a question of the degree of provocation. My life was at stake.

I've often acted as sword instructor. He won't be able to touch me: and I'll not hurt him. It will save explanations.

Oh, thank you: That's a cavalry man's proposal. I'm in the artilery: and I have the choice of weapons. If I go, I shall take a machine gun.

Significantly, Bluntschli does sometimes adopt Sergius' more literary manner, but not without wrenching it slightly out of shape. In the following examples, he uses antitheses, but in each case he sports with the figure instead of using it seriously as Sergius does. "I didn't ask the reason when you cried on: and I don't ask the reason now that you cry off," he tells Sergius. Here the rather forced juxtaposition of "cried on" and "cry off" sounds like conscious facetiousness on Bluntschli's part. A similar line, immediately following, has even more of a comic ring, and for the same reason: "I fight when I have to, and am very glad to get out of it when I haven't to." In much the same fashion, Bluntschli seems almost to parody the antithetical construction with the line: "You can always tell an old soldier by the inside of his holsters and cartridge boxes. The young ones carry pistols and cartridges: the old ones, grub." Here the omission of the verb in the second member, and the introduction of the thoroughly prosaic "grub," completely thwart the expected orderly completion of the figure.

In general then, Bluntschli's taste in words and word-order runs to the simple, not to say the austere. A no-nonsense professional soldier, accustomed to acting with rapidity and precision because his life and livelihood depend upon it, Bluntschli quite appropriately reveals habits of speech which reflect these qualities. He uses contractions, colloquialisms and short unadorned sentences because he is a man of business and these forms represent the most expeditious and efficient way of getting the job done. A man of Bluntschli's disposition simply has no time to seek out exotic terms or to embroider delicately balanced periods.

Sergius stands quite at the other pole, constantly selecting the supra-ordinary in language. Hence, the fundamental difference in the two characters – the difference so crucial to the comic action of the play – appears in the style of speech they employ just as surely as it appears in the opinions they voice and the actions they discharge. Sergius' allegiance to heroic, romantic patterns of behavior finds a counterpart in his marked preference for elevated patterns of language, while Blutschli's more mundane approach to to love and war finds its counterpart in his very earthy style.

Diction thus occupies a prominent position among the various elements which go to make up the comic power of the play. The exaggerated staginess of Sergius' mode of utterance, especially when contrasted with Bluntschli's homely prose, arouses the comic emotions because it constitutes a bearing-off from the linguistic course sensible men normally set themselves. Just as he deviates ludicrously in his conceptions of the nature of love and war, Sergius also deviates in his way of talking, and becomes more richly comic in proportion as he does so.

* * *

What Shaw does with Sergius resembles the method of literary satire proper, a method he has more closely approximated in the three short pieces already examined. It is important to notice also how the method here differs. In the straight parody, the object of ridicule is almost exclusively the original writer. Not so here. Shaw is not asking us to laugh at Byron and Pushkin, at least not to any significant degree; he is inviting us to laugh at Sergius and his real-life counterparts, for taking the language of Byron and Pushkin out of its proper sphere and carrying it over into life. It is only when thus misappropriated that the romantic style becomes ridiculous. Sergius does with the style of his favorite authors what Cashel Byron does with the style of Shakespeare, but with this important difference: Shaw means to say that there *are* such men as Sergius, though of course Shaw enlarges greatly upon what he finds in life, while Cashel Byron is sheer fantasy, conjured up to show how silly it *would* be *if* men talked like Shakespearean characters.

The method employed with Sergius is organically related to Shaw's most basic comic purposes. As already indicated, Shaw uses the comic form to ridicule attitudes which he considers outmoded, unrealistic and potentially pernicious. In order to point up the essential barrenness and sterility of the attitudes he wishes to criticize, he has their exponents voice them in the catchwords and formulas into which such attitudes tend to become frozen. Clichés of thought have a way of solidifying in clichés of language. Shaw recognized this and acted upon it, with the result that much of his social satire includes linguistic satire; he ridicules conventional mores by having his comic victims espouse these mores in the conventions of language most closely associated with them.

This intimate relationship between conventional thought and conventional language is a subject on which Shaw has characters comment in a remarkable number of instances. One of the most striking statements occurs in a little-known fragment of dialogue between Pilate and Jesus, which appears in the Preface to *On The Rocks*. Pilate has threatened to scourge his prisoner and Christ has made reference to the cruelty of such a measure, when the following exchange occurs:

PILATE: Leave out cruelty: all government is cruel; for nothing is so cruel as impunity. A salutary severity —

JESUS: Oh please! You must excuse me, noble Governor; but I am so made by God that official phrases make me violently sick. Salutary severity is ipecacuanha to me. I have spoken to you as one man to another; in living words. Do not be so ungrateful as to answer me in dead ones.

In *Great Catherine*, (1913) another ruler echoes Pilate's sentiments in almost exactly the same language; says Catherine: "A monarch, sir, has sometimes to employ a necessary and salutary severity —." Edstaston's reply makes the same point Jesus had made, though somewhat less elegantly; he cuts her off with "Quack! Quack! Quack!"

In yet another repetition of the same refrain, Julius Caesar, though himself a ruler, allies himself with Jesus and Edstaston in expressing a similar contempt for the cant of command: " ... a wise severity, a necessary protection to the commonwealth, a duty of statesmanship — follies and fictions ten times bloodier than honest vengeance."

The term "duty" which Caesar uses scornfully here is for Shaw almost a symbol of the whole network of artificial language which he so abhors; he shows his distaste for it in play after play. Elsewhere in *Caesar and Cleopatra* (1898) he has another character attack it. When a centurion declares: "I do my duty. That is enough for me," Appolodorus observes: " ... when a stupid man is doing something he is ashamed of, he always declares that it is his duty." The same idea appears in *The Admirable Bashville* (1901), where we hear:

MELLISH: Think of Nelson's words: England expects that every man —
CASHEL: Shall twaddle about his duty.

Though the word "duty" is not used, a similar thought finds expression in *The Devil's Disciple* (1897). Major Swindon declares that "the British soldier will give a good account of himself," and states his intention to "rely on the devotion of my countrymen." General Burgoyne effectively deflates this rhetoric by inquiring, "May I ask are you writing a melodrama, Major Swindon?"

In another case, it is the superior who is guilty of cant and a common soldier who gives the necessary rebuke. In *Press Cuttings* General Mitchener speaks habitually in officialese and The Orderly calls it "stuff you can get out of books." He contrasts his own rough-and-ready style with Mitchener's habitual artificiality: "It ain't polite," he says, "but it's English. What you say ain't anything at all." At one point, having failed to budge his most unmilitary Orderly with the proper command, "Right about face," Mitchener screams: "Get out of the room this instant, you fool; or I'll kick you out," which prompts the Orderly to observe: "I don't mind that, sir. It's human. It's English. Why couldn't you have said it before?"

These references to "melodrama" and "stuff out of books" have their counterpart in a line in *Heartbreak House* (1919), where artificial language is attributed to yet another source. Mangan, in attempting to convince Shotover that he will indeed marry Ellie, declares: "I never made up my mind to do a thing yet that I didn't bring it off. That's the sort of man I am; and there will be a better understanding between us when you make up your mind to that, Captain." Immediately following this manifesto we have:

SHOTOVER: You frequent picture palaces.

MANGAN: Perhaps I do. Who told you?

CAPTAIN: Talk like a man, not like a movy. You mean that you make a hundred thousand a year.

Shaw's intolerance of anyone who will not "talk like a man" also shows itself in *Back To Methuselah* (1920). When Conrad asks Franklyn if Joyce Burge has called him a liar, Franklyn answers: "No: I wish he had: any sort of plain speaking is better than the nauseous sham good-fellowship our democratic public men get up for shop use . . . ." In Part IV of the same play, *Tragedy of an Elderly Gentleman*, Shaw makes freedom from such "sham" one of the characteristics which distinguish the superior longlivers from the benighted shortlived who are to become extinct when Utopia has been achieved. Thus, in a conversation between representatives of the two groups we hear Zoo, a longliver, speak disdainfully of the "slavery of the shortlived to images and metaphors."

In another of Shaw's Utopian works, *The Simpleton of the Unexpected Isles* (1934), there is further criticism of empty verbiage. Iddy asks Maya to "speak to me like a human being," and Maya retorts: "That is how I speak to you; but you do not recognize human speech when you hear it: you crave for slang and small talk, and for ready made phrases that mean nothing. Speak from your soul . . . ."

An example of the sort of thing Maya has in mind occurs also in *Getting Married* (1908). Hotchkiss, writhing with unrequited love for Mrs. George, moans lugubriously: "Useless to prolong this agony. Fatal woman – if woman you are indeed and not a fiend in human form–;" she interrupts him with: "Is this out of a book? Or is it your usual society small talk?"

Don Juan also has little patience with catchwords and pat phrases; to the Devil, who has been trafficking in them, he protests: " . . . beauty, purity, respectability, religion, morality, art, patriotism, bravery, and the rest are nothing but words which I or anyone else can turn inside out like a glove."

All of this invective, (and this is but a sampling) put into the mouths of such a variety of characters, points unmistakably to a sustained animus on Shaw's part against the use of hollow form in language, against the mindless repetition of the standardized and codified. Whenever language becomes automatic, whenever it fails to function as a vehicle for the expression of the Life Force, Shaw has a spokesman on hand to deliver the appropriate rebuke.

In many plays, it is only a phrase or two which triggers a scornful remark about "stuff out of books." But in others, as we have seen in the case of Sergius, a character is made to spout formulas on something like a regular basis. Where this occurs, we may speak of linguistic satire. *Candida* (1895) written immediately after *Arms and The Man* offers additional examples.

C. E. Montague has said that, in *Candida*, Shaw " . . . dissected the general and respectable vice of living, not perhaps by phrases alone, but by unexamined phrases out of all proportion to reasoned beliefs or profound emotions." "By a proper train of incident," Montague explains, "Morell is winnowed and found to consist almost exclusively of branny phrases."[6]

Morell does indeed reveal a flair for rather empty sententiousness; as another critic puts it, he is a "master of rhetorical magniloquence, stuffed to his clerical collar with pulpit metaphors and the periods of conventional socialism . . . ."[7] Like Sergius, Morell appreciates, among other devices, the fine ring of a parallel series arranged in climactic order: "I shamed the guardians out of accepting your tender:" he tells Burgess. "I shamed the ratepayers out of letting them do it: I shamed everybody but you."

And to Marchbanks he cries: "Oh, if she is mad enough to leave me for you, who will protect her? Who will help her? Who will work for her? Who will be a father to her children?" But doubtless the finest example is an earlier speech to Marchbanks, which includes also a number of those "branny phrases" Montague mentions:

I will be your true brother in the faith. I will help you to believe that every stroke of your work is sowing happiness for the great harvest that all — even the humblest — shall one day reap. And last, but trust me, not least, I will help you to believe that your wife loves you and is happy in her home. We need such help, Marchbanks: we need it greatly and always. There are so many things to make us doubt, if once we let our understanding be troubled. Even at home, we sit as if in camp, encompassed by a hostile army of doubts. Will you play the traitor and let them in on me?

Though Morell never quite matches the transparent turgidity of this passage anywhere else in the play, other lines show him leaning in much the same direction. "A parson is like a doctor . . . " he tells his curate. "He must face infection as a soldier must face bullets." Later, echoing the threadbare cleverness of this observation, he tells Marchbanks: "Man can climb to the highest summits, but he cannot dwell there long."

These routine embellishments come from Morell in moments of comparative calm, when the practiced orator might be forgiven for falling easily into the formulas of his profession. But even when he has his strongest cues for passion, he seems unable to escape flaccid tumidity: "I had rather you plunged a grappling iron into my heart than given me that kiss," he groans to Candida. He avoids the straightforward and unadorned even in his all-important "bid" in the celebrated auction scene. Ever the master of the stately period, he declares:

I have nothing to offer you but my strength for your defence, my honesty of purpose for your surety, my ability and industry for your livelihood, and my authority and position for your dignity. That is all it becomes a man to offer to a woman.

To be sure, such affectations do not add up to a pronounced eccentricity. If not properly pointed by a skillful actor, they might in fact go unnoticed by all but close students of the play. But that Shaw intended some degree of ridicule of ministerial verbosity in having Morell talk in this fashion seems borne out by the stage directions as well as by comments of other characters. When Marchbanks asks Morell to tell Candida that the two of them have decided to make her choose between them, Morell replies: "I have nothing to tell her, except [*here his voice deepens to a measured and mournful tenderness*] that she is my greatest treasure on earth − if she is really mine." If the parenthesis here only hints that Morell is trying some of his platform magic on Candida, the comment appended to Candida's response makes an outright statement of the charge; Shaw says she speaks "coldly, offended by his yielding to his orator's instinct and treating her as if she were the audience at the Guild of St. Matthew." Elsewhere Candida speaks of his being "in love with preaching" and calls his sermons "mere phrases that you cheat yourself and others with every day."

Marchbanks also helps to underscore this aspect of Morell's character. He tells Prossy that he "can see nothing in him but words . . . ," berates Morell to his face for his "Everlasting preaching! Preaching! Words! Words! Words!," and tells Candida, after a protracted conversation with James, that he and her husband have been engaged in "a preaching match."

The fact that Marchbanks mocks himself as well as James in this last observation, points to another instance of linguistic satire in the play. For Marchbanks too is frequently guilty of verbal posturing. Though different from Morell's, his mode of utterance also represents a moderately ludicrous, artificial style − a fact that has all but escaped notice in the mass of commentary on the play. As Walter N. King has observed, "One of the oddest facets in criticism of *Candida* is . . . the general recognition that Morell's rhetoric smells of platitudes, while the rhetoric of Marchbanks goes all but unnoticed as the stalest effluvia of post-romantic jargon, forgivable only because of his almost incredible youth."[8]

Ironically, Marchbanks at one point displays his tawdry poeticisms while in the very act of condemning Morell for bombast. In answer to his antagonist's lengthy message about "sowing happiness" and reaping "the great harvest," Marchbanks asks: "Is it like this for Candida always? A woman, with a great soul, craving for reality, truth, freedom, and being fed on metaphors, sermons, stale perorations, mere rhetoric. Do you think a woman's soul can live on your talent for preaching?"

Though different in kind from Morell's "harvest" and "camp" metaphors, this chatter about "great souls" and "craving for reality" scarcely excels in quality. His opening shot in the prolonged battle with Morell is equally hollow: "You think yourself stronger than I am," he begins. "But I shall stagger you if you have a heart in your breast." Morell's mocking rejoinder suggests the spirit in which Shaw doubtless intended such heroics to be received.* "Stagger me, my boy," he replies.

But the quiet rebuke no more restrains Marchbanks than Marchbanks' jibes restrain Morell; he is soon soaring aloft again, on dangerously tattered wings. To Candida he offers:

... a tiny shallop to sail away in, far from the world, where the marble floors are washed by the rain and dried by the sun, where the south wind dusts the beautiful green and purple carpets. Or a chariot — to carry us up into the sky, where the lamps are stars, and don't need to be filled with paraffin oil every day.

He seems to be especially fond of the sky, for elsewhere he prates of coming "into heaven, where want is unknown," and of "standing outside the gate of heaven, and refusing to go in." His thoughts are again in the airy regions when he tells Morell that Candida "offered me all I chose to ask for, her shawl, her wings, the wreath of stars on her head, the lilies in her hand, the crescent moon beneath her feet."

This last outburst Morell describes as "poetic fripperies," another bit of debunking of the sort to which even Candida is later driven: "I would die ten times over sooner than give you a

---

* Some commentators have viewed Marchbanks' outpourings as a serious attempt on Shaw's part to write genuine poetic language, and have lauded or belittled the effort accordingly. Thus, Conor A. Farrington, deploring the lack of critical "ear" among the American writers on the drama, says writers "... can praise the cheap chintzy speeches of Marchbanks ...." ("The Language of Drama," *Tulane Drama Review,* V, Winter [1960], p. 70). To take these speeches seriously, whether to praise or censure them, seems to me entirely wide of the mark. Surely the more tenable position is to view them as deliberate travesties of poetic language.

moment's pain," Marchbanks protests." "With infinite contempt for this puerility," according to Shaw's stage direction, Candida replies: "Much good your dying would do me!" Eventually, even Marchbanks himself acknowledges his addiction to embellishment. When Morell, greatly agitated, seeks to learn what has passed between his wife and the young poet in their evening alone together, Marchbanks begins his account with "What happened! Why, the flaming sword . . . ," whereupon Morell "stamps with impatience" and Marchbanks yields, resuming with "Well, in plain prose, I loved her so exquisitely that I wanted nothing more than the happiness of being in such love." He also admits his posturing to Candida, though only after she has confronted him with it. In the course of their tête-à-tête he asks if he may "say some wicked things" to her and she says, "No. But you may say anything you really and truly feel. Anything at all, no matter what it is. I am not afraid, so long as it is your real self that speaks, and not a mere attitude: a gallant attitude, or a wicked attitude, or even a poetic attitude. I put you on your honor and truth. Now say whatever you want to." Thoroughly put off, Marchbanks can only reply: "Oh, now I can't say anything: all the words I know belong to some attitude or other . . . ."

* * *

As the examples seem to show, both men lapse very frequently into the clichés of their respective points of view, with Morell purveying the bromides of Christian socialism while Marchbanks traffics in the pink nebulae of adolescent poetasting. In both cases, however, verbal eccentricity scarcely passes the threshold of comic effectiveness. Compared to the extravagancies of style Sergius struts about in, the occasional departures of Morell and Marchbanks seem hardly noteworthy. True, Marchbanks does sometimes push his romantic outpourings to comic excess, as in the line, "Only horror, horror, horror," but more often than not his genuine anguish precludes a purely comic response to the excesses of his diction. Similarly, Morell now and again invites laughter with his canonical manner, but for the most part his peculiarities of utterance seem to remain just this side of genuine comic aberration.

The reasons for this are not far to seek. However one interprets this notoriously enigmatic play, it appears that both Marchbanks and Morell grow and change and learn in the course of the action. Accepting for the sake of convenience and illustration the classic interpretation to the effect that Marchbanks, Morell and Candida correspond, respectively, to the realist, idealist and Philistine of *The Quintessence of Ibsenism*, it is clear that at the end of the play Morell has had his idealistic view of marriage profoundly shaken, if not totally shattered, while Marchbanks has been confirmed in the realistic view towards which he had been merely groping. Whatever the terms one selects to describe it, some such process of change occupies an essential place in the action. In that fact lies the reason for the relatively slight development given the comic deviations incipient in the respective styles of the two characters. Total commitment to demonstrably aberrant habits of expression tends to brand a character as incapable of change. Confronted with a character firmly locked in a markedly outlandish way of talking, we are naturally led to suppose that he will remain pretty much as we find him, not only as concerns his manner of speaking, but in all other aspects of his makeup as well. For this reason, the playwright who concerns himself with the psychological development of his characters must necessarily shun obtrusive verbal fixations. Jonas Barish elucidates this home truth of comic representation as follows:

The moment psychological realism comes into play, with its premise of growth . . . language sheds its high eccentricity, its contorted peculiarity, and becomes a pliant instrument for registering change. . . . It is always those characters incapable of growth . . . who pipe away in a strange . . . falsetto, and always the more "organic" figures . . . who speak in a relatively neutral, transparent style.[9]

Thus, Marchbanks and Morell, both clearly "organic" characters, speak in a "relatively neutral" style capable of registering the change so important to the action of the play. Both characters have their little oddities of diction but these necessarily remain fragmentary, so as to obviate any strong suggestion of automatism which would impede the process of growth.

In *Captain Brassbound's Conversion*, Shaw again ventures into the realm of linguistic satire but the preoccupation with psychological change again precludes extensive employment of the device.* The play has to do with the folly of vengeance; as Chesterton says, "Shaw here treats vengeance as something too small for man — a monkey-trick he ought to have outlived, a childish storm of tears which he ought to be able to control."[10] In the brigand Brassbound, Shaw depicts a man who has for years nurtured the dark dream of revenge, only to discover in the end the foolishness of the whole idea. When Lady Cicely makes him aware of the absurdity of his position, he at first protests that she has "belittled" his "whole life" to him, but by the play's end he welcomes his conversion and humbly thanks its author.

As Bentley has shown, this action constitutes an "inversion" of conventional stage melodrama.[11] Shaw first presents the audience with a typical hero, hot in pursuit of the enemy who has wronged his mother and stolen his birthright. He invites the spectator's sympathy for the character and then yanks the carpet from under him by exposing his "hero" as a bit of an ass after all. In this fashion, Shaw punctures not only his character but those members of the audience who have identified with the character's point of view.

Such an action obviously depends heavily upon a careful rendering of Brassbound. If the trick is to work, Brassbound must be convincing enough in the early part of the play to invite sympathy, and yet just extreme enough in his views to make probable, and palatable, his later exposure at the hands of Lady Cicely. In short, he must be neither a complete fool nor thoroughly admirable.

This requirement extends to matters of diction as well as to other aspects of character. Accordingly, we find Brassbound employing the language of the stage avenger only occasionally, and then only in its less obtrusive forms.

---

* As psychological realism is of the essence of Shavian comic dramaturgy, it follows that few of the central characters display pronounced eccentricities of style. For an examination of the "neutral" style they employ instead, see Chap. VI.

His earliest utterances, though hardly remarkable, reveal a rather self-conscious laconicism, which suggests introspection, dedication to purpose, fires banked down inside, deep melancholia and other familiar earmarks of a man aware of his central position in the unfolding of high drama. As Shaw says, he is "a man of few words . . . and much significance." In his parting conversation with the hated Sir Howard, at the end of Act I, his speech fairly vibrates with lugubrious "significance":

BRASSBOUND: Sir Howard Hallam: I advise you not to attempt this expedition.

SIR HOWARD: Indeed! Why?

BRASSBOUND: You are safe here. I warn you, in those hills there is a justice that is not the justice of your courts in England. If you have wronged a man, you may meet that man there. If you have wronged a woman, you may meet her son there. The justice of those hills is the justice of vengeance.

SIR HOWARD [*faintly amused*]: You are superstitious, Captain. Most sailors are, I notice. However, I have complete confidence in your escort.

BRASSBOUND [*almost threateningly*]: Take care. The avenger may be one of the escort.

SIR HOWARD: I have already met the only member of your escort who might have borne a grudge against me, Captain; and he was acquitted.

BRASSBOUND: You are fated to come, then?

SIR HOWARD [*smiling*]: It seems so.

BRASSBOUND: On your head be it.

Brassbound's use of Sir Howard's full name in the first line, the ponderous explicitness and weighty formality of the "justice" speech, his use of the terms "avenger" and "fated," and his final oracular pronouncement "On your head be it," combine to give this sequence a "mysterioso" quality which needs only a few accompanying bass notes on the piano to make it worthy of Pixérecourt himself. Small wonder that Shaw instructs the actor playing Sir Howard to respond with smiles and faint amusement.

Faint amusement must surely be the intended response also to certain other of Brassbound's lines. "All the wealth of England shall not ransom you," he grandly informs Sir Howard. Asked what he hopes to gain, if not ransom, he announces: "Justice on a thief and a murderer." Becoming more and more eloquent as this confrontation progresses, he charges Sir Howard with exacting vengeance upon "many and many a poor wretch in the dock." Cataloguing the wrongs visited upon his mother by Judge Hallam, Brassbound even makes reference to one of the perennial features of nineteenth-century melodrama: " . . . you drove her from your doors," he tells the judge. No less redolent of the speech of a Ten-twen'-thirt' protagonist is the line: "Even the price you offer for your life is to be paid in false coin." With similar bombast, he says of his family ties with Sir Howard: "If I thought my veins contained a drop of his black blood, I would drain them empty with my knife." But doubtless the most damning line he utters, the line which most clearly reveals his affinity with stage avengers, is the declaration: "I will teach other scoundrels to respect widows and orphans."

In all these lines, and others like them, Brassbound uses the overcharged, purple-tinted diction of conventional blood-and-thunder drama. In so doing, he takes on a comic dimension which, added to, and harmonizing with, other elements of his character, helps to make him the butt of Shaw's ridicule of the revenge motive in human affairs.

Shaw returned to this subject some ten years later, in *Misalliance* (1910), creating a character strikingly similar to Brassbound. Gunner, (also identified as "The Man," "John Brown," and "Julius Baker,") slinks onto the stage, like Black Paquito before him, gun in hand, bent upon judging and executing John Tarleton, for the supposed "betrayal" of his dead mother; he even has crumpled photographs of the wronged lady in his pocket, just as Brassbound has. As might be expected, his speech lets us in on the joke almost from the start. Avenger and victim have hardly met when the following exchange occurs:

THE MAN: . . . Are you trying to put me in the wrong, when you have to answer to me for a crime that would make every honest man spit at you as you passed in the street if I were to make it known?

TARLETON: You read a good deal, don't you?

THE MAN: What if I do? What has that to do with your infamy and my mother's doom?

TARLETON: There, you see! Doom! Thats not good sense; but it's literature. Now it happens that I'm a tremendous reader: always was. When I was your age I read books of that sort by the bushel: the Doom sort, you know.

A minute or so later, Tarleton restates the point when he tells the would-be Young Norval: "Judging from your conversational style, I should think you must spend at least a shilling a week on romantic literature."

Tarleton's slighting appraisal is based on abundant evidence, as a random sampling of Gunner's lines makes clear: "Thank heaven I've not a drop of your vile blood in my veins;" "Monster! Without conscience! Without even memory! You left her to her shame—" "Are women to be ruined with impunity?" He even uses one direct quotation, in a line reminiscent of the borrowings used in *Dark Lady*; flourishing "Before and After" portraits of his hapless mother, he asks Tarleton to "Look here, upon this picture and on this."

Having heard such ravings, we can readily agree with and laugh with Tarleton when he tells his pursuer: " . . . You want to be the hero of a romance and to get into the papers. Eh? A son revenges his mother's shame. Villain weltering in his gore. Mother: look down from heaven and receive your unhappy son's last sigh."

This and similar assaults soon persuade Gunner to leave off his assumed *persona*, but he has hardly done so when he takes up another, equally recognizable and equally ridiculous. The Free Library, where he has learned to play Nemesis, has evidently supplied him also with a shelf of Socialist literature, because he is soon showing himself as much the master of the reformer's argot as he was of the avenger's. Thus, having eavesdropped on Tarleton's daughter Hypatia as she makes some rather indecorous proposals to a young man who has caught her fancy, Gunner tattles on her to her parents, framing his denunciation in the catchphrases of a Hyde Park harangue: "*I* can tell you where Hypatia is. I can tell you where Joey is. And I say it's a scandal and an infamy. If people only knew what goes on in this so-called respectable house it would be put a stop to. These are the morals of our pious capitalist class! This is your rotten bourgeoisie!" As usual, Shaw underscores the joke by pointedly identifying the style he is lampooning; when Mrs. Tarleton takes offense at Gunner's outburst; deploring "such language," her husband attempts to reassure her by explaining that "it's not bad language: it's only Socialism." But Gunner is not to be restrained. He goes on to denounce Hypatia as "One of the smart set! One of the bridge-playing, eighty-horse-power, week-ender set! One of the johnnies I slave for!" and to prophesy that she and her class are doomed: "The writing is on the wall. Rome fell. Babylon fell. Hindhead's turn will come." Further heckling from his captive audience, including the threat of arrest, only pricks him on to greater rhetorical excesses:

GUNNER . . . I never asked to be let off. I'm ashamed to be free instead of taking my part with the rest. Women — beautiful women of noble birth — are going to prison for their opinions. Girl students in Russia go to the gallows; let themselves be cut in pieces with the knout, or driven through the frozen snows of Siberia, sooner than stand looking on tamely at the world being made a hell for the toiling millions. If you were not all skunks and cowards you'd be suffering with them instead of battening here on the plunder of the poor.

Following this peroration, Tarleton finally cows him, though only momentarily, by subjecting his effusions to the same hard-headed and sharp-tongued analysis with which he had greeted his earlier ranting; he tells him to "cut the cackle." Eventually, Gunner's passion is spent, his attitude mellows, and he desists, though even in yielding he "cackles:" "I'm so full of your bourgeois morality that I let myself be shocked by the application of my own revolutionary principles."

Such speeches fully qualify Gunner for admission to the ranks of those who deal in second-hand language. Gunner has already been compared here to Brassbound, who is certainly his closest counterpart in the plays. The two might also be thought of as belonging to a larger group which would include Sergius and Marchbanks, since all four characters employ a style which could be loosely described as "literary," and more specifically identified as "romantic," "poetic," or "melodramatic."

Such a category might also include General Boxer Bridgenorth of *Getting Married* (1908). In his protracted and bootless wooing of Lesbia, Boxer sometimes has recourse to a style which another Shaw character, (She, in *How he Lied to Her Husband*) calls "flapdoodle." He employs it when he tells Lesbia: "You have thawed the long-frozen springs." Lesbia cuts short another such flight to point up its absurdity:

GENERAL: The heart has its preferences, Lesbia. One image and one only, gets indelibly—

LESBIA: Yes. Excuse my interrupting you so often; but your sentiments are so correct that I always know what you are going to say before you finish.

Boxer's brother Reginald is also familiar with, and tired of, his pronouncements; Boxer is expostulating with Reginald for striking his wife when Reginald interrupts to deliver mockingly the speech he knows is on the tip of his brother's tongue: "The man that would raise his hand to a woman, save in the way of a kindness, is unworthy the name of Bridgenorth."

But Boxer's foolishness can only rarely be identified as the parroting of sentimental novels; he voices the sentiments found in such works but our laughter is more at the attitudes themselves than at a recognizable vocabulary and syntax. The satire, in short, is only minimally linguistic.

Much the same is true of Roebuck Ramsden, of *Man and Superman* (1903). When Tanner advises him that the cultivation of a "little impudence" is the way to attract attention, Ramsden haughtily declines the suggestion, in terms which provoke the immediate scorn of Tanner:

RAMSDEN: I have no—

TANNER: You have no desire for that sort of notoriety. Bless you, I knew that answer would come as well as I know that a box of matches will come out of an automatic machine when I put a penny in the slot: you would be ashamed to say anything else.

Tanner also mocks Ramsden, much like Reginald mocking Boxer, by delivering a speech he thinks Ramsden is about to give. When the supposedly "fallen" Violet is revealed to be present in Ramsden's house, Tanner exclaims: "What! Under Ramsden's sacred roof! Go and do your miserable duty, Ramsden. Hunt her out into the street. Cleanse your threshold from her contamination. Vindicate the purity of your English home. I'll go for a cab."

Tanner is fair enough in all of this; Ramsden is a prig; he considers Violet's supposed premarital indisposition a fate worse than death and condemns Tanner's book as infamous, admitting with his next breath that he has not read it. But his priggishness does not frequently reveal itself in clichés of language, as Tanner suggests. It is significant, for example, that Ramsden does not actually use the phrase "Fate worse than death," though he conveys precisely that thought; Octavius asks if Violet is dead and Ramsden replies: "I am not sure that it is not even worse than that." Tanner catches this and later makes fun of it ("Dreadful, appalling. Worse than death, as Ramsden says."), but even this does not amount to ridicule of language so much as ridicule of an attitude.

Shaw gives another character in the play, Hector Malone *fils*, the same "elevated moral sentiments" which animate Ramsden, but again stops short of giving him the whole catalogue of phrases which regularly house such attitudes. Only once does Hector display the rococo style of a Brassbound or Sergius; he tells Violet, who has called Tanner a beast, that "he's all right: he only needs the love of a good woman to ennoble him."

It would no doubt be idle to inquire too closely into Shaw's reasons for going no further in this direction with Ramsden and Malone, but two possibilities might be suggested. For one, he had already done it with Sergius and Brassbound, and could have added little to the point developed so thoroughly and effectively in those instances. For another, both these characters have minor roles to play in the grand design of *Man and Superman* and could not be allowed to claim too much interest lest they shift the comic focus away from Tanner and Ann.*

* Boxer and Gunner, of *Getting Married* and *Misalliance* respectively, are in a somewhat different position. Both of these plays are loose-jointed and episodic in structure and can therefore contain a variety of comic types of roughly equal prominence.

Man and Superman reveals yet another touch of linguistic satire, of a type not found elsewhere in the plays. Tanner himself now and again takes a leaf from Sergius' book to intone such fustian as "Abyss beneath abyss of perfidy!" and "Infamous, abandoned woman! Devil!" This may at first seem a glaring inconsistency in the man who has ridiculed Ramsden, but one realizes that Tanner is employing the style tongue-in-cheek. It is for him a light-hearted affectation, somewhat reminiscent of Father Keegan putting on the brogue for his chat with the Grasshopper in *John Bull*. This is clear from everything else we know about Tanner's character and seems to be revealed explicitly in one particular line: "OH! Unfathomable deceit! Double crossed!," where the slang expression calls deliberate attention to the conscious artificiality of the first ejaculation. In giving Tanner this trick of speech, Shaw reveals again the method of work he had employed with his use of dialect: the habit of taking a comic device, holding it up to the light and turning it every which way until its every facet has been observed and appreciated.

* * *

Mimicry of the emotion-charged language of romantic literature and stage melodrama appears in brief flashes in other major plays but it seldom extends to more than an isolated line or so. Sergius, Brassbound, and Marchbanks are the only major characters who exhibit it, and Boxer, Gunner, and Ramsden the only characters in major plays who reveal it to any noteworthy extent. The device in its most complete form belongs almost exclusively, in fact, to the first decade of Shaw's work. After *Captain Brassbound's Conversion*, in 1899, it is given sustained attention only in three of the short "trifles," *How He Lied to Her Husband* (1904), *Passion, Poison, and Petrifaction* (1905) and *Overruled* (1912); even in these works it is exaggerated to the point of buffoonery, arousing easy farcical laughter instead of the more thoughtful amusement it provokes in the other plays.

All of the characters examined thus far, except Morell — and Gunner in his role of socialist firebrand — have been caught employing styles which bear a loose relation to one another, in that all can be traced to a provenance in literature vaguely identifiable as "romantic." Morell and the second Gunner belong to another cluster of characters whose modes of utterance can also be assigned a unifying similarity. The ambience of the language of these characters is perhaps best labeled political, though no single term adequately embraces the heterogeneity of the category; it includes all of the shadings of the language of public life and public affairs, whether the immediate source of the style be journalism, the forum, political tracts, or official correspondence; it accommodates the clichés of every persuasion: socialistic, imperialistic, liberal, and conservative. It consists, in short, of the sort of thing Franklyn Barnabas has in mind in the speech already quoted: "the nauseous sham goodfellowship our democratic public men get up for shop use," except that it is not limited to the cant of *democratic* public men.

We have already seen Pilate, Catherine, and others using offending phrases of this type and heard Caesar's abhorrence of them. In the *Pilate-Jesus* fragment and in *Great Catherine* there are few examples. *Caesar and Cleopatra* (1898) does have somewhat more and is the earliest play to use the device after *Candida* (1895), where Morell's pulpit eloquence is satirized. It is Caesar's British secretary, Brittanus, in contrast to Caesar, who displays a predilection for officialese. When Caesar declares bluntly to the assembled dignitaries of Egypt: "I am badly in want of money," Brittanus, "disapproving of these informal expressions," feels he must translate for him: "My master would say that there is a lawful debt due to Rome by Egypt, contracted by the King's deceased father to the Triumvirate; and that it is Caesar's duty to his country to require immediate payment." This insistence on using the contortions of diplomatic communication is never carried quite so far anywhere else in the play, but flashes of it appear here and there in Brittanus' frequent references to "duty" and "honor." The most comic of these includes also one of the play's many deliberate anachronisms; when Caesar tells the Egyptians that they shall have Cyprus "for the sake of peace," Brittanus sanctimoniously adds "Peace with honor," thereby "unconsciously anticipating a later statesman," as Shaw tells us.

If such characters as Bill Walker and Enry Straker are preliminary studies of the Doolittles, Brittanus might be considered an
exercise in preparation for the *chef d'oeuvre* that is Tom Broadbent. To this protagonist of *John Bull's Other Island* (1904),
Shaw devotes his greatest expenditure of ingenuity in the carica-
turing of forensic circumlocution. Julius Bab called Broadbent a
character " . . . who has every prospect of becoming immortal as
the prototype of the average Englishman;"* a more precise
description would make him the prototype of British officialdom;
he is Shaw's definitive portrait of John Bull.

Like the other major figures whose characterization involves
linguistic satire, Broadbent is comic in ways additional to and
probably more important than the strictly verbal. Like any comic
character, Shavian or otherwise, designed to carry the weight of
the playwright's more important comic meaning, Broadbent is
primarily laughable for his habits of thought and feeling, rather
than his style of speech: speech, after all, is largely an accidental,
in the logician's sense of that term, and is in that respect not
greatly superior to baggy pants or crossed eyes in the high-low
scale of comic materials. Broadbent is comic in his essence; he has
a comic soul, as it were, not just an absurd "body."

But, again, external trappings, including language, can function
as the conspicuous outer sign of ludicrous aberrations within.
Broadbent's mannered mode of utterance works in just that way,
to guide our perceptions unerringly inward toward his comic center.

At only slight risk of hyperbole, it might be said that Broadbent has not a single stylistic ploy of which he can rightly claim
to be the natural progenitor. His conversation consists almost
exclusively of political and sociological cant, most of it skimmed
from the stagnant waters of journalism and parliamentary debate.

He begins to sport his out-at-the-elbows finery in one of his
earliest speeches. When Tim Haffigan, lying outrageously, tells
him that he is a "teetotaler," Broadbent immediately mounts the
platform: "So am I, of course, I'm a Local Optionist to the

---

* " . . . *der alle Aussicht hat, unsterblich zu werden als der Typ des
Durchschnitts-Englanders . . . .*" (Julius Bab, *Bernard Shaw* (Berlin,
1926), p. 242).

backbone. You have no idea, Mr. Haffigan, of the ruin that is wrought in this country by the unholy alliance of the publicans, the bishops, the Tories, and The Times," this last a ringing phrase of the type which he might have read in the *Times* itself. Though the occasion is an informal interview in the privacy of Broadbent's office, what follows for the next page and more is not a conversation but an oration by Broadbent, punctuated intermittently by polite murmurs from Haffigan, whose attention is engaged much more strongly by the oversized tumbler of whiskey he has just mooched. A casual reference to Ireland leads Broadbent to expatiate on the Irish Question, which he presently leaves to deal vigorously with the more general question of England's relations with small nations. At least, that is what he seems to be talking about; his address is so cluttered with rhetorical flotsam as to be nearly unintelligible. " . . . the last remnants of national liberty," "an Englishman's first duty," "it is under their heel that Ireland is now writhing," "patriotic young men who avenged the wrongs," and "every civilized man must regard murder with abhorrence," comprise only a partial list of the stock phrases which jostle each other in the speech. The spectator can readily second Haffigan when he declares at one point: "Sure I know every word youre goin to say before yev said it."

After a short space of more relaxed discourse, Broadbent is off again; with all the cloying patronization of a present-day Southern aristocrat describing "the Nigra," he delivers his analysis of the Irish National character: " . . . I saw at once that you were a thorough Irishman, with all the faults and all the qualities of your race: rash and improvident but brave and goodnatured; not likely to succeed in business on your own account perhaps, but eloquent, humorous, a lover of freedom, and a true follower of that great Englishman Gladstone." As if fearful of having omitted one of the obligatory phrases, he returns to the subject a few lines later, imploring Haffigan to "come with me and help break the ice between me and your warmhearted, impulsive countrymen."

Broadbent's preposterous exhibition of so many of the most shopworn figures of public advocacy, pitted against Haffigan's feigned but exotic brogue, make the scene a duel of "dialects" which rivals in comic inventiveness the later Donnybrook between the elder Haffigan and Broadbent's man, Hodson.

But the scene is not exceptional, as far as Broadbent is concerned. He adheres to the hortative mode, with brief and infrequent hiatuses, throughout the play. The result is consistently comic, as several other characters help us to see. Thus, when Broadbent, with irrepressible ingenuousness, assures his Irish-born partner, Larry Doyle, that "Home Rule will work wonders under English guidance," Larry, "his face twitching with a reluctant smile," asks: "Tom: why do you select my most tragic moments for your most irresistible strokes of humor?" Broadbent's subsequent insistence that he was "perfectly serious," can hardly be doubted; he remains so throughout, while dispensing the most patent blather. Doyle also offers us a somewhat more detailed, and equally accurate analysis of his partner: " . . . I never stop wondering at that blessed old head of yours with all its ideas in watertight compartments, and all the compartments warranted impervious to anything that it doesn't suit you to understand." Doyle might have added that, in each compartment, Broadbent has also stored away for easy access, all the phrases that go with the ideas.

When Broadbent later strews such phrases about the Irish countryside with uncontained prodigality, some of Doyle's countrymen also take his measure. Father Dempsey, having just been treated to a particularly flavorful sample of his eloquence, states his estimate of Broadbent's chances for a parliamentary seat with the simple directness of a simple man: "Well, he hasn't much sense, God help him; but for the matter o' that, neither has our present member."

Barney Doran, another member of the local establishment summoned to sit on Broadbent's qualifications for the district's seat in Parliament, also deflates Broadbent, in our eyes if not in the eyes of those assembled. Though unintentional and indirect, Doran's sally is no less effective than Doyle's or Father Dempsey's. When Broadbent announces that he cannot speak about Home Rule "without using the language of hyperbole," Doran happily misconstrues the meaning of "hyperbole" and with a

worldly-wise nudge to Broadbent whispers "Savin Fadher Dempsey's presence, eh?"

But Broadbent needs no hecklers to "write him down an ass."
He condemns himself out of his own mouth with unstinting regularity. His hackneyed euphuisms are so numerous and so extrava-
gant, and the settings in which he parades them so obviously
unsuited, that we are on to him before any of his fellow characters point the finger of ridicule.

Shaw nevertheless makes doubly sure that we will see Broadbent as he sees him by contriving two episodes which set the
character before us with great force and clarity. If we were to ask
what occasion of human discourse is most decidedly inappro-
priate to the employment of the Epideictic style, we might very
well choose the proposal of marriage. Shaw apparently asked such
a question and accordingly wrote a scene which finds Broadbent
in that delicate situation. True to form, he lugs at least part of his
rhetorical baggage with him onto the loveseat, to the discomfiture
and bewilderment of his heart's desire, Nora Reilly. There is a
dim but unmistakable patina of the diplomatic note encrusted on
his request for Nora's hand: "You must not think I am going to
press you for an answer before you have known me for twenty-
four hours. I am a reasonable man, I hope; and I am prepared to
wait as long as you like, provided you will give me some small
assurance that the answer will not be unfavorable." The same
aura hangs about further protestations of affection: " . . . I daresay you have noticed that in speaking to you I have been putting
a very strong constraint on myself, so as to avoid wounding your
delicacy by too abrupt an avowal of my feelings. Well, I feel now
that the time has come to be open, to be frank, to be explicit.
Miss Reilly: you have inspired in me a very strong attachment.
Perhaps, with a woman's intuition, you have already guessed
that." Given the impossible stuffiness of such an avowal, it is no
wonder that Nora responds with: "Why do you talk to me in that
unfeeling nonsensical way?" She had already caught the inappro-
priateness of his tone from his earlier overture, which had pro-
voked her to declare: " . . . I sometimes think you're not quite
right in your head, Mr. Broadbent, you say such funny things."

But no amount of chiding will swerve Broadbent from his
rhetorical rut; his ignorance of himself is complete, as he reveals

in protesting to her that he is "a plain unemotional Englishman, with no powers of expression." His very considerable, if inveterately tacky, powers of expression, continue to show in this most curious of love scenes, as he goes on to speak of her "Irish delicacy," to praise her for being "really most delicately womanly," and to promise her that theirs will be a "solid four-square home." The scene perhaps reaches its highest point of comic power when Broadbent delivers an opinion on the proprieties governing physical displays of affection. When Nora, who had cried on his breast in an earlier scene, suggests that a man ought never to let another woman touch him after one has honored him in that way, he agrees, but with reservations, couched, inevitably, in forensic metaphor: "One should not. One ought not, my dear girl. But the honest truth is, if a chap is at all a pleasant sort of chap, his chest becomes a fortification that has to stand many assaults: at least it is so in England."

In all fairness, it should be noted that Broadbent does occasionally descend the rostrum in his tête-à-tête with Nora. He does eventually manage to say quite directly: "I love you. I want you for my wife," but his inability to shed his robes of state altogether, for a scene of the most private nature, is a damaging index of his addiction to grandiloquence.

An even stronger index of his bizarre linguistic proclivities emerges from a second episode which Shaw contrives for that purpose. When Broadbent is drafted to stand for the Rosscullen parliamentary seat, he is given an occasion for speech-making which, if it does not justify the degree of rhetorical artifice he brings to it, is at least more legitimately related to that style, in kind, than is the ordinary business and social intercourse for which he elsewhere employs it. The absurdity of his earlier and later verbal posturing is therefore given added comic emphasis when that style, used deliberately in a *bona fide* political context, turns out to be hardly a whit more turgid than it had been when used for responses to the small talk of the locals. Shaw notes in a stage direction that Broadbent begins his remarks to the Rosscullen delegation by "collecting himself for a political deliverance." The hint is hardly necessary; what follows, all of which is designed to awe the rustic kingmakers with his political acumen, is a pastiche of shoddy convention-hall oratory immediately familiar to any but the most reclusive citizen of a free society. His opening period is typical:

BROADBENT: . . . All I can say is that as an Englishman I blush for the Union. It is the blackest stain on our national history. I look forward to the time — and it cannot be far distant, gentleman, because Humanity is looking forward to it too, and insisting on it with no uncertain voice — I look forward to the time when an Irish legislature shall arise once more on the emerald pasture of College Green, and the Union Jack — that detestable symbol of a decadent Imperialism — be replaced by a flag as green as the island over which it waves — a flag on which we shall ask for England only a modest quartering in memory of our great party and of the immortal name of our grand old leader.

The inclusion of this direct parody of campaign floridity adds a second prong to the fork of Shaw's satire. Put into the mouth of an office seeker addressing his would-be constituents, it takes to task the stylistic confections of politicians generally, censuring such abominations of language even when employed in the business of vote-getting and public suasion. Elsewhere in the play, the comic point of Broadbent's verbal eccentricities is rather different. In such scenes as the Haffigan interview and the wooing of Nora Reilly, we laugh not only at the mawkishness of the style itself but at Broadbent for being so imbecilic as to employ it in such contexts. Both comic points depend for their effectiveness on our recognition of the style; in both instances we are invited to laugh at language itself.

There is an objection that might be raised to this way of looking at Broadbent. It might be argued that it is wide of the mark to place so much emphasis on his speech style, since the character of such a man could not very well be represented dramatically at all without endowing him with language of this type; the style *is* the character, and this being so, it is only in a manner of speaking that we laugh at language. This may be readily granted; the only point being urged here is that this particular dramatic character owes his comic nature to the prior existence, outside the play, of a unique configuration of language, the nature of which we must know and recognize if the character is to have his proper comic effect upon us. The same thing is clearly not true of numerous other comic characters, whether in the plays of Shaw or those of other dramatists, and that fact allows us to speak of Broadbent and others as examples of a particular method of work — a method involving a very special use of language.

A final observation must be made about Tom Broadbent, lest his character be badly misrepresented here. Even in his most clownish moments he does not excite in us what is usually called punitive laughter. An utterly silly man he most certainly is, but a despicable one never. Shaw sees to it that our view of him shall be something like Larry Doyle's view, who finds him an exasperating driveller but a good soul nonetheless. There is, after all, no malice in the man, and his peculiar brand of idiocy does nobody any harm, not even himself. He is not even hypocritical; his wholesale appropriation of the gaudiest political gimcrackery is carried on with pristine innocence; he never means to cheat, could not if he wanted to — so patently inferior is the quality of his wares — and realizes no profit from the trade he carries on, save perhaps a deep personal satisfaction in what he blithely supposes to be his devilishly clever way with words. Whatever we may expend in the way of sharply critical laughter is directed not at Broadbent himself, but at those real-life functionaries of whom he reminds us, charlatans whose linguistic legerdemain *is* meant to dupe the unwary.

In plays written after *John Bull*, Shaw frequently includes large blocks of such linguistic satire, though the theme is never again given the degree of prominence it enjoys in that play. A year after *John Bull* he allows it a few measures in *Major Barbara* (1905). That Broadbent and his ilk are still on his mind he reveals in a speech he gives to Lady Britomart. Upbraiding Cholly Lomax for his obtrusive dependence on slang, she gives him this advice:

In good society in England, Charles, men drivel at all ages by repeating silly formulas with an air of wisdom. Schoolboys make their own formulas out of slang, like you. When they reach your age, and get political private secretaryships and things of that sort, they drop slang and get their formulas out of *The Spectator* and *The Times*. You had better confine yourself to *The Times*. You will find that there is a certain amount of tosh about *The Times*; but at least its language is reputable.

Though she never says so, Lady Britomart may well have learned about the silly formulas of the *Times* by listening to her own son, Stephen. In any case, Stephen uses them, as Undershaft is quick to detect. An unconscionable prig, Stephen's ceaseless declarations of principle frequently have a suspiciously pat ring to them. Having inspected his father's munitions works, he gives the establishment his approval with: "I have satisfied myself that the business is one of the highest character and a credit to our country." There is also something of the tone of a leading article in his speech when he remonstrates with Undershaft for claiming that the industrialists rule England:

Really, my dear father, it is impossible to be angry with you. You don't know how absurd all this sounds to me. You are very properly proud of having been industrious enough to make money; and it is greatly to your credit that you have made so much of it. But it has kept you in circles where you are valued for your money and deferred to for it, instead of in the doubtless very old fashioned and behind-the-times public school and university where I formed my habits of mind. It is natural for you to think that money governs England; but you must allow me to think I know better.

The exchange immediately following this pronunciamento finds Stephen spouting additional formulas:

UNDERSHAFT: And what does govern England, pray?

STEPHEN: Character, father, character.

UNDERSHAFT: Whose character? Yours or mine?

STEPHEN: Neither yours nor mine, father, but the best elements in the English national character.

Undershaft's incisive particularizing of the word "character" unmasks Stephen's highly conventional use of the term. More strikingly, Undershaft greets the "English national character" line with a comment which seems to tie Stephen's prating directly to Lady Britomart's observation, made only a few moments earlier, about The *Times* and The *Spectator*. "Stephen," he says mischievously, "I've found your profession for you. You're a born journalist. I'll start you with a high-toned weekly review. There!"

Other samples of Stephen's prose validate Undershaft's appraisal. In stating his misgivings about his Father's womb-to-tomb care of his workers Stephen parrots to the letter the argument of numberless foes of Socialism: "Well, I cannot help thinking that all this provision for every want of your workmen may sap their independence and weaken their sense of responsibility . . . ." He knows by rote also the proper answer to make when Undershaft laughs at his vaunted certainty about the nature of right and wrong: "I pretend to nothing more than any honorable English gentleman claims as his birthright."

To be sure, these are little more than faint pipings, compared to Broadbent's trumpet blasts, but Stephen's jangling melodies are clearly played from the same score.

Stephen has a close ally in Johnny Tarleton of *Misalliance* (1910). A militant Philistine, the younger Tarleton has all of Stephen's fondness for moral dogmatism. "If you ask me," he declares to Lord Summerhays, "I like a man who makes up his mind once for all as to what's right and what's wrong and then sticks to it. At all events you know where to have him." When Summerhays fails to embrace this view, Johnny goes on to insist that "You can draw a line and make other chaps toe it. That's what I call morality."

Another remarkable similarity with Stephen and with other characters we have met, appears in the play's opening dialogue between Johnny and Lord Summerhays' son, Bentley. When Johnny refers to Bentley's father as "The strongest man England has produced in our time—" Bentley remarks contemptuously: "You got that out of your halfpenny paper." The lengthy reply this provokes from Johnny is an unabashed profession of vintage imperialism:

I don't set up to be able to do anything but admire him and appreciate him and be proud of him as an Englishman . . . . For twenty-five years he kept a place twice as big as England in order: a place full of seditious coffee-colored heathens and pestilential white agitators in the middle of a lot of savage tribes. And yet he couldn't keep you in order. I don't set up to be half the man your father undoubtedly is; but, by George, it's lucky for you you were not my son. I don't hold with my own father's views about corporal punishment being wrong. It's necessary for some people; and I'd have tried it on you until you first learnt to howl and then to behave yourself.

But Johnny is not simply Broadbent or Stephen over again. The significant thing about this passage is that while Johnny's sentiments are readily classifiable, the language in which they are couched is not; it is, by and large, his own. He is perhaps indebted to his halfpenny paper for "seditious coffee-colored heathens," but most of his vocabulary is convincingly spontaneous and natural, even colloquial. He pointedly does not use, for example, the phrase "wise severity," which Shaw ridicules on three other occasions, but conveys precisely that thought. Relevant to the present discussion, his case seems to prove that it is possible to satirize a given political philosophy without also satirizing the style most closely associated with it. And this, of course, argues strongly for deliberate artifice on Shaw's part in his characterization of Broadbent and others.

* * *

That same artifice is not strongly in evidence again until *Augustus Does his Bit*, written in 1916. In wildly irreverent burlesque of the homefront war effort, Lord Augustus Highcastle, recruiting officer in Little Pifflington, attempts to marshall the resources of that community by badgering its lethargic inhabitants with the slogans of official directives and the rallying cries of the patriotic press. "Our gallant fellows perishing in the trenches" are invoked no less than five times, the populace is warned that "the Hun is at the gate," and, of course, every man is repeatedly admonished to "do his bit."

When not thus urging his comrades onward, Augustus avails himself of another ready-made style. Greeted by "The Lady" as "The Great Lord Augustus," he demurs modestly with: "I should not dream of describing myself so, madam; but no doubt I have impressed my countrymen — and [*bowing gallantly*] may I say my countrywomen — as having some exceptional claims to their consideration." When this performance provokes admiration, he openly admits the source of his fluency: "It would be strange indeed if, after sitting on thirty-seven Royal Commissions, mostly as chairman, I had not mastered the art of public expression. Even the Radical papers have paid me the high compliment of declaring that I am never more impressive than when I have nothing to say."

On one of those Commissions, Augustus could almost have met a character from *Back to Methuselah*, written just four years later. Joyce Burge, who appears in *The Gospel of the Brothers Barnabas*, is described in the play as a "flaming fraud" and the epithet could hardly be more apt. Conrad observes that Burge "has talked so much that he has lost the power of listening," and one is tempted to add, "even to himself." For surely no man who listened to himself could go on talking as Burge talks. Though the war has been over for two years, its rhetoric is still fresh in his mind and quick to his tongue. In one of his recollections of those palmy days – when he had been the prime minister – he easily outdoes even Augustus' tumidity; defending his association with coalitions, to which he claims to be opposed in principle, he gives this rationale for having formed two of them: "Why? Because we were at war. That is what you fellows never would realize. The Hun was at the gate. Our country, our lives, the honor of our wives and mothers and daughters, the tender flesh of our innocent babes, were at stake. Was that a time to argue about principles?"

He recalls the Hun's presence at the beleagured gate at least one other time, pointing out in almost the same breath that it had been necessary to "rise above party" in those trying times. The Hun never got through the gate of course, as he also reminds his listeners, in a speech rife with that mixture of false modesty and unmitigated pomposity at which Augustus excelled. When Franklyn, challenging Joyce's political credentials, asks "What are you?" he declares: "I am, if I mistake not, Joyce Burge, pretty well known throughout Europe, and indeed throughout the world, as the man who – unworthily perhaps, but not quite unsuccessfully – held the helm when the ship of state weathered the mightiest hurricane that has ever burst with earth-shaking violence on the land of our fathers."

All of this occurs, not at a party rally attended by thousands, but before an audience of five in the Barnabas sitting room, though Burge's excesses could hardly be excused even on an occasion of the most phrenetic political ritualism. Like Broadbent, Burge is constitutionally incapable of plain speaking, whatever the situation in which he finds himself. Unlike Broadbent, however, he seems not altogether oblivious of the fact that he is trafficking in shopworn phrases. His party rival and predecessor in office, Lubin, reminds him that he fairly revelled in his wartime stewardship, and subtly accuses him of infatuation with the slogans of the Great Offensive: "How you enjoyed yourself over that business, Burge! Do you remember the Knock-Out Blow?" Not at all chagrined, Burge accepts this characterization and confirms it, reminiscing with obvious relish over another resounding call to arms: "It came off: don't forget that. Do you remember fighting to the last drop of your blood?"

Lubin also takes Burge's stylistic measure in another exchange. When Burge, fulgurating as usual, tells Lubin that "The great movement of mankind, the giant sweep of the ages, passes you by and leaves you standing," Lubin silences him with: "It leaves me sitting, and quite comfortable, thank you. Go on sweeping. When you are tired of it, come back; and you will find England where it was, and me in my accustomed place . . . ."

As in the case of Shaw's other full-scale caricatures of artificial language, the joke really requires no such explicit pointing. In his very first utterance, Burge makes a display which can leave no doubt about the sort of buffoonery Shaw means us to see in him. In an outrageous hotchpotch of Shakespearean sublimity unparalleled even in Shaw's broadest short plays, Burge attempts to flatter Conrad Barnabas, a professor of biology, with a panegyric to that science: "There is nothing like biology. 'The cloud-capped towers, the solemn binnacles, the gorgeous temples, the great globe itself: yea, all that it inherit shall dissolve, and, like this influential pageant faded, leave not a rack behind.' Thats biology, you know: good sound biology."

Reference has been made to Shaw's contention, set down elsewhere in *Methuselah*, that the slavery of public men to puffed-up metaphor — of which Burge represents an extreme case — will be eliminated eventually by the Life Force, in its relentless drive toward perfection. It is significant, in light of this, that the President of the British Isles in the next play of the Pentateuch, *The*

Thing Happens, is relatively free of the malady. Burge-Lubin, a descendant of the Burge and Lubin clans, 250 years removed, has barely a trace of it. He prattles of England's invention of parliament as "her peculiar and supreme glory," and prates of the English as "a race divinely appointed to take charge," but these are lapses which can be forgiven a man in his august position. For the most part, he talks sanely enough, owing no doubt to the strain of Lubin blood in his veins, since his forbear on that side had also been decently restrained in his dependence on rhetoric.

Matters have improved still more in Part IV of the play, *Tragedy of an Elderly Gentleman*. By this time at least, thirty years later, there have evolved a sizeable number of individuals who enjoy sufficient longevity to have freed themselves entirely from the evasions of official utterance. So complete is their transcendence in this area, that they find the patter of the shortlived simply incomprehensible. This makes for a lively scene of word-play between The Woman, Fusima, representing the new order, and The Elderly Gentleman, one Joseph Popham Bolge Bluebin Barlow, O. M., "formerly Chairman of the All-British Synthetic Egg and Vegetable Cheese Trust in Baghdad, and now President of the British Historical and Archeological Society, and a Vice-President of the Travellers' Club." The breakdown of communication begins almost immediately; "Daddy," as Fusima calls him, explains his presence in Ireland, the island stronghold of the longlivers:

THE ELDERLY GENTLEMAN: . . . I have come here on a pious pilgrimage to one of the numerous lands of my fathers. We are of the same stock, you and I. Blood is thicker than water. We are cousins.

THE WOMAN: I do not understand. You say you have come here on a pious pilgrimage. Is that some new means of transport?

THE ELDERLY GENTLEMAN: I find it very difficult to make myself understood here. I was not referring to a machine, but to a — a — a sentimental journey.

THE WOMAN: I am afraid I am as much in the dark as before. You said also that blood is thicker than water. No doubt it is; but what of it?

THE ELDERLY GENTLEMAN: Its meaning is obvious.

THE WOMAN: Perfectly. But I assure you I am quite aware that blood is thicker than water.

THE ELDERLY GENTLEMAN: We will leave it at that.

When Fusima continues to challenge his presence, the misunderstandings multiply. When Daddy asks if he is trespassing and Fusima fails to understand, he obligingly "explains," in a fashion which leads only to her increased bewilderment: "Is this land private property? If so, I make no claim. I proffer a shilling in satisfaction of damage (if any), and am ready to withdraw if you will be good enough to shew me the nearest way." At this, Fusima confesses that she has understood not a word, whereupon The Gentleman protests that he is "speaking the plainest English."

These *malentendus* recur throughout the play, reaching the point of highest development in The Elderly Gentleman's confrontation with Zoo, another young woman summoned to deal with him because she is a mere fifty-six years old, and therefore perhaps better capable of understanding what her elders can only regard as his impenetrable lallation. But Zoo fares not much better, though in extenuation it must be said that he subjects her to formidable tests. At the height of a discussion about the benefits of individual longevity, Daddy delivers a paean to the civilization of the shortlived, worthy of Broadbent or Burge:

THE ELDERLY GENTLEMAN: Young woman: you are mistaken. Shortlived as we are, we — the best of us, I mean — regard civilization and learning, art and science, as an ever-burning torch, which passes from the hand of one generation to the hand of the next, each generation kindling it to a brighter, prouder flame. Thus each lifetime, however short, contributes a brick to a vast and growing edifice, a page to a sacred volume, a chapter to a Bible, a Bible to a literature. We may be insects; but like the coral insect we build islands which become continents: like the bee we store sustenance for future communities. The individual perishes; but the race is immortal. The acorn of today is the oak of the next millennium. I throw my stone on the cairn and die; but later comers add another stone and yet another; and lo! a mountain.

He is about to go on to further conceits, when Zoo cuts him short by "laughing heartily at him," and calling him "a funny little

man, with your torches, and your flames, and your bricks and
edifices and pages and volumes and chapters and coral insects and
bees and acorns and stones and mountains." Despite his protest
that these are "metaphors merely," she insists on interpreting the
passage literally, concluding that he means to say his ancestors
were "about a quarter of an inch high" and that his distant prog-
eny will have reached the height of three or four miles. Told that
he didn't mean that, she responds with a judgement upon him
that may be taken for Shaw's own: "Then you didn't mean anything."

Not until civilization has progressed to *As Far as Thought Can
Reach*, in Part V of the play, are all who speak without meaning
anything finally bred out of the race, though even some of
Daddy's fellow shortlivers, Napoleon and the British Envoy, had
shown themselves capable of a promising straightforwardness. In
the Utopia with which Shaw concludes the play, only the children are allowed to indulge a talent for the figurative, and even
they for the briefest of times, since their span of youth is but
four short years, their childhood and early adolescence having
been spent in the eggs from which they hatch at about age seven-
teen. Thus, when Acis reaches the threshold of maturity he looks
back at his amorous idyll with Ecrasia with complete contempt
and upbraids her for "calling my limbs fancy names and mapping
me into mountains and valleys and all the rest of it . . . ." So
complete, in fact, is the evolution, that the most advanced
Ancients have escaped from the treacheries of language altogether, into a Nirvana of pure thought.

In thus envisioning with apparent pleasure a state of human
existence freed from *all* language, Shaw moves into regions where
many will not wish to follow. Joseph Wood Krutch has said that
Shaw here depicts "human nature and human society proceeding
along a path of evolution which renders both unrecognizable by,
and rather dubiously attractive to, those of us who are still domi-
nated by old-fashioned human nature and rather doubtful about
our desire to be quite so drastically changed."[12] Whatever may
be true of other features of Shaw's Elysium, few will welcome his
banishment from it of even the most legitimate uses of poetic
invention.

But Shaw's wordless paradise is still a long way off in the other plays we have been considering, and in others yet to come, and we need have no qualms about applauding his satire of such malefactors as Sergius and Broadbent.

*   *   *

Chaplain de Stogumber of *Saint Joan* (1923) perhaps deserves inclusion in the roll-call of such characters, if only because he sheds additional light on the technique Shaw uses with the others. As one of the play's staunchest defenders of the feudal system, he relies at least occasionally on some of the catchphrases of the political apologist. When his countryman Warwick, who is always refreshingly direct in stating his opinions, observes with gentle mockery that the Chaplain will favor a policy of "England for the English," de Stogumber misses Warwick's amusement and unblushingly adopts the phrase and other's like it: "Certainly England for the English goes without saying: it is the simple law of nature. But this woman denies to England her legitimate conquests, given her by God because of her peculiar fitness to rule over less civilized races for their own good."

But despite the similarity revealed here, de Stogumber differs from Augustus and company in a most crucial way: he is, quite simply, not funny. The reasons for his failure to amuse us make clear what Shaw has had to do with the other characters to keep them within the pale of the strictly comic. Unlike all his predecessors, de Stogumber is in a position to do great damage with his chauvinistic phrase-mongering; it is all directed against Joan herself, who is the conscious object of our greatest sympathetic concern. As already pointed out in the case of Broadbent, the other characters we have met in no way jeopardize anyone whose fortunes are a matter of importance to us. They operate in a vacuum, in a world where their foolishness has no perceptible consequences. Burge, for example, is out of office when we see him, and we are not allowed to even speculate about the disasters his conduct of the war might have caused. Were Shaw to put before us a mutilated survivor from among those "gallant fellows in the trenches," our attitude toward Burge would change rapidly into something like our attitude toward the rather despicable de Stogumber.

This device of deliberately obliterating, or at the very least obscuring, the painful consequences of a character's eccentricity, is of the essence of comic method, as most theorists have observed. In one of the very earliest formal inquiries into the nature of the laughable, Plato stated the case in terms which are especially appropriate here; equating "ignorance of self" with the whole spectrum of human folly, he finds this trait laughable, *except* in those in positions of power, where it becomes "hateful and ugly"[13] as in the case of de Stogumber.*

In subsequent plays, Shaw returns at least part way along the road to comic treatment of official utterance, though none of the plays of his last quarter-century contain anything as extensive as the best samples thus far encountered.

This is somewhat surprising, considering that three of the seven full-length plays of the later period have exclusively political settings and themes. *The Apple Cart* (1929), the next play after *Saint Joan*, is subtitled "A Political Extravaganza;" save for a short boudoir "Interlude" between Acts I and II, and two other incidental vignettes, the action centers entirely upon two meetings of the British Cabinet, in which we are introduced to the King, the Prime Minister, the President of the Board of Trade, the Foreign, Colonial, and Home Secretaries, the Chancellor of the Exchequer, the Postmistress-General and the Power-Mistress General. Even one of the short scenes outside the cabinet room, in the chambers of the King, includes a formal confrontation of King Magnus and the American Ambassador. For the purposes of Shaw's demonstrated interest in the speech peculiarities of the governing class, this roster of dignitaries in high council assembled amounts almost to an embarrassment of riches.

That very fact may account for Shaw's neglect of the device in this play; he could not very well give the trait to all these characters, and any choice of one or the other could only be arbitrary.

In any case, he does relatively little with it. Instead, he moves the language of his statesmen in the opposite direction, to make a very different joke, though still a linguistic one. One of the most

---

* Naturally I do not mean to suggest that Shaw faltered in his delineation of de Stogumber; he clearly does not intend him to be funny and so proceeds accordingly.

conspicuous comic features of the cabinet's deliberations is that they are carried on, not with the studied decorousness one expects of such a body, but in a style remarkable for its plainness, not to say slanginess. The members address each other with nicknames and diminutives (Postmistress Amanda is "Mandy," Pliny of the Exchequer is "Plin") and make their points with the help of such forceful expressions as "mind your own business," "no need to rub it in," and "that's got him." Only Boanerges, President of the Board of Trade, objects to this, pointing the joke for us in doing so. Boanerges is a captain of labor, a self-made man from the ranks and a newcomer to the Cabinet. As is usual with parvenus he has an exaggerated concern for the proprieties required of the class to which he has recently gained admission. He therefore remonstrates with his colleagues in the strongest terms for their frequent lapses in etiquette: "I say, let us be dignified. I say, let us respect ourselves and respect the throne. All this Joe and Bill and Nick and Lizzie: we might as well be hobnobbing in a fried fish shop. The Prime Minister is the prime minister: he isn't Joe." His recriminations fall on deaf ears, however, and the atmosphere of the fish shop is pretty well maintained throughout.

Only King Magnus speaks in a truly becoming fashion, and, most of the time, the Prime Minister. There are hardly more than two occasions when the Broadbent syndrome shows itself, and both times it is laughed out of court. Ambassador Vanhattan is one of the offenders; so encumbered is he in the formulas of his calling, that it is all Magnus can do to worm out of him the nature of his mission. Dispatched to advise the King that America has decided to rejoin the British Empire, he must first dawdle about, informing the Queen grandly that she need not leave the room, because "Whatever may be the limits of your privileges as the consort of your sovereign, it is your right as an Englishman to learn what I have come here to communicate." Magnus understandably considers it his right as well, and after a time politely urges him to "tell us as succinctly as possible what has happened." But even in the face of a kingly rebuke, Vanhattan goes on like a twentieth-century Osric, asking leave to "recall the parable of the prodigal son." Magnus regally bids him to forbear, but he recalls the parable anyhow: "The prodigal, sir, has returned to his father's house. Not poor, not hungry, not ragged, as of old. Oh no. This time he returns bringing with him the riches of the earth to the ancestral home." He finally does succeed in delivering his message, but observes the last jot and tittle of verbal protocol until he leaves the presence.

The only other significant example of this sort of thing in the play is Prime Minister Proteus' farewell tribute to Magnus, delivered in response to the King's announcement of his abdication. Shaw puts us in a properly irreverent frame of mind for the speech in two ways, just before it begins. Assured that Magnus is in earnest about abdicating, Proteus allows that "There is nothing more to be said," whereupon Amanda observes, "That means another half hour at least." Shaw also introduces the speech with a stage direction informing us that Proteus "rises and becomes the conventional House of Commons orator":

PROTEUS: My friends, we came here to a meeting. We find, alas! that the meeting is to be a leavetaking. [*Crassus sniffs tearfully*] It is a sad leavetaking on our part, but a cordial one. [*Hear Hear from Pliny*]. We are cast down, but not discouraged. Looking back to the past with regret, we can still look forward to the future with hope. That future has its dangers and its difficulties. It will bring us new problems; and it will bring us face to face with a new king. But the new problems and the new king will not make us forget our old counsellor, monarch, and — he will allow me to say — comrade.[*Hear Hears ad libitum*]. I know my words will find an echo in all your hearts when I conclude by saying that whatsoever king shall reign—

At this point, Amanda, who has barely kept countenance throughout, finishes the sentence with "You'll be the Vicar of Bray, Joe," throwing the assembly into complete disorder and ending the performance.

On The Rocks (1933), is subtitled "A Political Comedy," and like *The Apple Cart* it deals almost exclusively with the deliberations of statesmen and would-be statesmen. But like *The Apple Cart* also, the play ridicules only occasionally the entrapment of functionaries in the argot of their profession. The chief exemplar is the play's central character, Sir Arthur Chavender, the British Prime Minister. He reveals the tinge right from the start; confronted with a series of remonstrances for his failure to lift the country out of economic depression, he finds it impossible to deal with the topic without repeated references to the "revival of trade;" in the space of a few minutes he has:

They think because I'm Prime Minister I'm Divine Providence and can find jobs for them before trade revives.

... I intend to call a conference in March next on the prospects of a revival of trade . . . .

Do you suppose I would not revive trade and put an end to it all tomorrow if I could?

Some of them even hold that trade is already reviving.

But though he also leavens his remarks to colleagues and constituents with such phrases as "contrary to English instincts," and "the inexorable laws of political economy," his informal discourse is reasonably free of officialese. It is in his prepared statements — whether for the House of Commons or for others of the numerous assemblies he is called upon to address — that he treats verbal communication as a process of wiring together various machine-tooled parts which he has put by for the purpose in carefully ticketed containers. We never see him actually functioning on the platform, but we are made privy to his rehearsals, and the techniques of composition revealed in those moments brand him vividly. In its combination of studied prettiness and vacuity, the following passage resembles more the twittering of birds than the language of men:

"My Lords and gentlemen: you are not theorists. You are not rhapsodists. You are no longer young" — no, damn it, old Middlesex won't like that. "We have all been young. We have seen visions and dreamt dreams. We have cherished hopes and striven towards ideals. We have aspired to things that have not been realized. But we are now settled experienced men, family men. We are husbands and fathers. Yes, my lords and gentlemen: husbands and fathers. And I venture to claim your unanimous consent when I affirm that we have found something in these realities that was missing in the ideals. I thank you for that burst of applause: which I well know is no mere tribute to my poor eloquence, but the spontaneous and irresistible recognition of the great natural truth that our friends the Socialists have left out of their fancy pictures of a mass society in which regulation is to take the place of emotion and economics of honest human passion." Whew! that took a long breath. "They never will, gentlemen, I say they never will. They will NOT [*he smites the table and pauses, glaring round at his imaginary hearers*]. I see that we are of one mind, my lords and gentlemen. I need not labor the point." Then labor it for the next ten minutes. That will do. That will do.

Many features of the passage contribute to its satiric power but of primary importance among them are Sir Arthur's blithe certainty about where the applause will come and his reminder to himself to labor a point which he has just said does not need laboring. Both strokes point to an employment of language almost totally removed from the normal function of thought-transferral; in them, Sir Arthur is seen to regard speechmaking as an occasion upon which the speaker makes certain prescribed sounds guaranteed to evoke certain other prescribed sounds from auditors; that the sounds shall convey meaning is a requirement imposed neither by the speaker nor his auditors.

Though Sir Arthur's malady is no further advanced than in the other cases already examined, Shaw undertakes on this occasion to have a cure affected. The character identified simply as "The Lady" is Shaw's physician, and her diagnosis is precisely what it might have been had she been summoned to attend one of Sir Arthur's predecessors in office, Burge or Proteus. Sir Arthur treats her to a sample of his platform style, and there follows a discussion which represents Shaw's most explicit and most impassioned indictment of official utterance – indeed a kind of summation of all that Shaw implies in his delineation of the earlier characters of this type:

THE LADY: As I listen to you I seem to hear a ghost preparing a speech for his fellow ghosts, ghosts from a long dead past. To me it means nothing, because I am a ghost from the future.

SIR ARTHUR: That's a curious idea. Of course if there are ghosts from the past there must be ghosts from the future.

THE LADY: Yes: women and men who are ahead of their time. They alone can lead the present into the future. They are ghosts from the future. The ghosts from the past are those who are behind the times, and can only drag the present back.

SIR ARTHUR: What an excellent definition of a Conservative! Thank Heaven I am a Liberal!

THE LADY: You mean that you make speeches about Progress and Liberty instead of about King and Country.

SIR ARTHUR: Of course I make speeches: that is the business of a politician. Don't you like speeches?

THE LADY: On the Great Day of Judgment the speechmakers will stand with the seducers and the ravishers, with the traffickers in maddening drugs, with those who make men drunk and rob them, who entice children and violate them.

SIR ARTHUR: What nonsense! Our sermons and speeches are the glories of our literature, and the inspired voices of our religion, our patriotism, and − of course − our politics.

THE LADY: Sermons and speeches are not religion, not patriotism, not politics: they are only the gibbering of ghosts from the past. You are a ghost from a very dead past. Why do you not die your bodily death? Is it fair for a ghost to go about with a live body?

The Lady goes on to conclude that Sir Arthur is "dying of an acute want of mental exercise," and though Sir Arthur vigorously protests the diagnosis, she offers to restore his health by making him a patient at her retreat in the Welsh mountains, where he will be subjected to a regimen of "No newspapers, no letters, no idle ladies. No books except in the afternoon as a rest from thinking." Of this last stipulation, Sir Arthur asks, "How can you think without books?" a query which places him solidly in the company of all the plagiarists of the preceding plays.

Other ideas set forth in the scene are also intimately related to the overall pattern of linguistic satire found in the plays. In one such, there is a clear echo of Lady Britomart's observation about the formulas of The *Times*; Sir Arthur has been arguing that he and his fellow public men have all developed superior minds through their training at Harrow and Oxford; The Lady replies: "You mean that they can all be trusted to say the same thing in the same way when they discuss public affairs."

The Lady also analyzes Sir Arthur's problem in familiar terms in her farewell to him: "I guarantee that in a fortnight you will begin to think before you talk. Your dead mind will come to life. I shall make a man of you. Goodbye."

We are not permitted to witness the therapy applied during that fortnight, nor do we see, directly, its results, but we do learn that The Lady's treatment has worked. When Act II opens, Sir Arthur has returned from his two weeks in Wales and has made a speech which was like no other speech he ever made in his life. The reactions, pro and con, of his ministers and supporters assure us of that. Sir Broadfoot Basham, Commissioner of Police, states the case most succinctly: "It's amazing. I could have sworn that if there was a safe man in England that could be trusted to talk and say nothing, to thump the table and do nothing, Arthur Chavender was that man. What's happened to him? What does it mean? Did he go mad at the sanatorium, do you think? Or was he mad before that woman took him there?"

We are also given strong confirmation of Sir Arthur's metamorphosis in one of his own remarks. When Sir Dexter Rightside, his Foreign Secretary, regales him with precisely the sort of verbiage we heard Sir Arthur rehearsing before his convalescence, Sir Arthur ridicules the performance, and does so in terms which direct our thoughts deliberately back to his own earlier transgressions. Warned by Sir Arthur that the world is moving and may break whatever gets in its way, Sir Dexter replies: "Nothing has broken so far except the heads of the unemployed when they are encouraged by your seditious rot to rebel against the laws of nature. England is not breaking. She stands foursquare where she always stood and always will stand: the strongest and greatest land, and the birthplace of the noblest imperial race, that ever God created." Arthur's debunking response is: "Loud and prolonged cheering. Come! let us both stop tub-thumping and talk business."

The fact that Sir Arthur is thus rehabilitated makes him an appropriate character with whom to end this survey of Shaw's use of linguistic satire. In any case, he is the last Shaw character to embody the device in any marked degree. The few remaining plays offer occasional snatches of dialogue related to the subject, but they add nothing substantial to the pattern traced here.

That pattern, observable in varying degrees in works spanning nearly the whole of Shaw's career as a playwright, is a vital component of his comic machinery, a component which functions organically in the dramatic representation of Shaw's view of man and society. That comic view has already been characterized here as a vision of conflict between those who respond to the prompting of "healthy impulse" and those who allow themselves to become puppets of "artificial system." The intimate relationship between this thematic substructure of the plays and the kind of linguistic satire we have been examining is perhaps apparent from all that has already been said. The relationship is described for us in the clearest terms in a speech Shaw gives to Aubrey in *Too True to Be Good*. In Act II, Sweetie has been speaking with utter frankness about her past amorous affairs and The Patient (Miss Mopply) has replied that she cannot bear to listen to such "frightful coolness;" Aubrey offers an eloquent defense of Sweetie:

We all have — to put it as nicely as I can — our lower centres and our higher centres. Our lower centres act: they act with a terrible power that sometimes destroys us; but they don't talk. Speech belongs to the higher centres. In all the great poetry and literature of the world the higher centres speak. In all respectable conversation the higher centres speak, even when they are saying nothing or telling lies. But the lower centres are there all the time: a sort of guilty secret with every one of us, though they are dumb.

. . . .

That is what makes Sweetie almost superhuman. Her lower centres speak. Since the war the lower centres have become vocal. And the effect is that of an earthquake. For they speak truths that have never been spoken before — truths that the makers of our domestic institutions have tried to ignore. And now that Sweetie goes shouting them all over the place, the institutions are rocking and splitting and sundering. They leave us no place to live, no certainties, no workable morality, no heaven, no hell, no commandments, and no God.

There is no mistaking Shaw's preference here for those in whom the lower centers speak; it is against those in whom the higher centers speak, the Brassbounds and the Broadbents, that he repeatedly directs his satire.

CHAPTER V

Automatism and Word-Play

The speech of ordinary social intercourse often assumes forms as absurdly artificial in their way as those of any literary or professional idiom. Daily discourse abounds in empty expletives, meaningless tag ends of phrase and, above all, in formulas: fixed, set, rigidly circumscribed expressions which appear automatically whenever the need arises to deal verbally with certain social situations. There are formulas for wedding receptions, for wakes, for holidays, for the birth of a baby — in short, for all the regularly recurring "occasions" of human existence. At such times, language tends to lose its function as the vehicle of thought and becomes instead a sort of reflex action; the speaker becomes an automaton, responding in a predetermined way to a specific stimulus.

Obviously a certain amount of this linguistic automatism serves a useful function and warrants little censure even from the most zealous apostles of vitalism. To insist that a man find a fresh, spontaneous, truly individual way of reacting to every newborn baby presented for his appraisal, would be to demand an expenditure of effort out of all proportion to the requirements of the situation. Newborn babies, like cocktail parties, promotions, and appendectomies, represent basically indistinguishable, "stock" stimuli, which justify stock verbal responses: "he looks like his father," "I had a very nice time," etc.

Moreover, even where the stimulus does seem to warrant a special, particularized response, as when the baby is hopelessly homely or the promotion clearly undeserved, society tends to excuse, if not indeed to demand, the usual polite reaction, preferring dishonesty to the tiffs and squabbles truthfulness would produce. Even so stern a critic of social hypocrisy as Molière seems to grant the necessity of this kind of dissimulation. In *The Misanthrope,* Philinte argues:

In certain cases it would be uncouth
And most absurd to speak the naked truth;
With all respect for your exalted notions,
It's often best to veil one's true emotions.
Wouldn't the social fabric come undone
If we were wholly frank with everyone?[1]

Shaw also concedes this point, it would seem. In *Pygmalion,* the fatuous Miss Eynsford Hill expresses the wish that "people would only be frank and say what they really think!" "Lord forbid!" Higgins replies. "What they think they ought to think is bad enough, Lord knows; but what they really think would break up the whole show. Do you suppose it would be really agreeable if I were to come out now with what I really think?"*

But automatism in speech cannot always claim the excuse of convenience or of social necessity, and where it cannot, it may constitute comic aberration. At any rate, dramatists have long made capital of it, in one form or another. In the earliest plays, direct satire of the tendency toward automatic repetition of phrases in everyday discourse does not appear, but something closely resembling it does. Aristophanes recognized the comic potential of word-repetition and used the device often, as in the well-known contest scene of *The Frogs,* where Aeschylus accuses Euripides of framing his prologues "so that each and all fit in with a . . . 'bottle of oil' " and proceeds to prove it as follows:

EURIPIDES [quoting]: Aegyptus, sailing with his fifty sons, as ancient legends mostly tell the tale, touching at Argos

---

* Nevertheless, Higgins does say "what he really thinks" on a number of occasions and is somewhat ridiculous in consequence, as is Alceste. Their very failure to use the formulas of social amenity represents a comic departure from sensible conduct.

AESCHYLUS: Lost his bottle of oil.

EURIPIDES: Hang it, what's that? Confound that bottle of oil!

DIONYSUS: Give him another: let him try again.

EURIPIDES: Bacchus, who, clad in fawnskins, leaps and bounds with torch and thyrsus in the choral dance along Parnassus

AESCHYLUS: Lost his bottle of oil.[2]

The exchange continues through several more quotations, the "bottle of oil" refrain popping up each time with machine-like regularity.

In a similar passage in *Twin Menaechmi,* Plautus also exploits the comic potential of mechanistic utterance:

MENAECHMUS I: [to wife]: Has one of the slaves been cutting up? Are the maids or the manservants answering back? Tell me. They won't get away with it.

WIFE: Nonsense!

MENAECHMUS I: She's really mad. I don't like this much.

WIFE: Nonsense!

MENAECHMUS I: You must be angry with one of the servants.

WIFE: Nonsense!

MENAECHMUS I: Well, are you angry with me, then?

WIFE: Now that's not nonsense.

MENAECHMUS I: What the devil: I haven't done anything.

WIFE: More nonsense again![3]

Commenting on this and similar passages in Roman comedy, Duckworth writes: ". . . these repetitions illustrate well Bergson's theory of the mechanical as a source of laughter, but such mechanical regularity may also be considered a form of incongruity which derives its effect chiefly from the unexpected."[4] Whatever the psychological basis of our pleasure in it, the device has proved its effectiveness in the work of the greatest comic writers.[5] Molière uses it when he has Organ repeat the question, "And Tartuffe?" and Shakespeare does the same thing in the trial scene of *The Merchant of Venice,* where first Shylock, and then Gratiano repeatedly cry "O Learned Judge."

Examples of this rather elementary use of repetition are not hard to find in Shaw's plays. Sergius does it in *Arms and The Man* with a series of lines in which he boasts of his indomitability: "I never withdraw," "I am never sorry," "I never apologize." Each time, Shaw instructs the actor to deliver the line with a tone of "measured emphasis" and to fold his arms, thereby underscoring the mechanical element. This element is given still more obvious pointing when Bluntschli, having caught on to Sergius' habit, and seeing him fold his arms in the telltale preparatory way, steals his thunder and tells Louka, who has demanded that Sergius apologize: "It's no use. He never apologizes." The fact that Shaw describes Sergius on this occasion as being "like a repeating clock of which the spring has been touched," makes clear that he is fully conversant with the comic possibilities of mechanical repetition.

The trial scene in Act III of *Captain Brassbound's Conversion* offers another example. In the course of the proceedings, Drinkwater repeatedly interjects comments of varying degrees of imbecility; six times his shipmate Redbrook attempts to silence him with "Shut up, you fool!"

In none of these cases does mechanical repetition constitute the major or even an important technique of comic characterization. The wife of Menaechmus, Organ, Sergius and the others are all comic for other reasons, if they are otherwise comic at all, and these occasions are the sole occasions, or nearly so, on which their dialogue falls into the pattern.

But comic dramatists, some of these same dramatists among them, have at other times made fixation upon various words and phrases the single most conspicuous comic trait of certain characters. They have depicted characters who consistently punctuate their utterances with this or that favored expression or who habitually clutter their speeches with a variety of superfluous words automatically introduced. As with other matters of comic diction, Jonson is doubtless the foremost practitioner of the technique. Wasp, of *Bartholomew Fair,* represents a typical example, with his predilection for short, interrogatory clauses at the ends of statements, as in:

Whetston has set an edge upon you, has he?
You are the Patrico! are you?
Why, say I have a humour not to be civil; how then?[6]

In Jonson's plays, such verbal nervous tics serve as signs of highly particularized comic eccentricity; for him, mechanistic twitches are a manifestation of special varieties of folly, not directly applicable to men in general. In recent years, Samuel Beckett and Eugene Ionesco have indicted men at large for mindless automatism in the use of words. They have fixed their attention upon those stock phrases so much in evidence in daily conversation and by exaggerating the frequency of their repetition have satirized their use. In an article significantly entitled "The Tragedy of Language," Ionesco comments on this species of human folly and tells how he sought to dramatize it in *The Bald Soprano:*

[The play] is, above all, concerned with a kind of universal bourgeoisie, the petty bourgeoisie being the personification of accepted ideas and slogans, the ubiquitous conformist. His automatic use of language is, of course, what gives him away. The text of *The Bald Soprano* . . . , composed of ready-made expressions and the most tired clichés, made me aware of the automatic quality of language and human behavior, "empty talk," speaking because there is nothing personal to say, the absence of inner life, the mechanical aspect of daily existence, man bathing in his social environment, becoming an indistinguishable part of it.[7]

Shaw seems to look both ways in his treatment of "empty talk," backward to Jonson's use of it as a device of highly individualized eccentricity and forward to Ionesco's condemnation of the more general human tendency toward the automatic in discourse.

There is an excellent representative of the first type in Shaw's first play, *Widowers' Houses* (1892). William de Burgh Cokane sounds most of the few comic notes to be heard in this predominantly sombre work, and he does so primarily through his distinctly idiosyncratic handling of the language.

Cokane never contents himself with simply making a statement; he runs off batches of statements. He deals in job lots, and he turns them out with the clickety-click efficiency of a precision turret-lathe, all the syntactical knurls and grooves identically duplicated. Cokane subscribes to the principle that if one statement of the case will do the job, two or three or four restatements will do it that much better. The following examples make up only a portion of the whole:

Recollect yourself, Harry: presence of mind, presence of mind!

Dont mention it, my dear sir: dont mention it.

Act responsibly, Harry: act responsibly.

Ah, that is going too far, my dear sir, too far.

Finished, dear boy, finished. Done to a turn, punctually to the second.

True: true. Quite true.

His affection for his daughter is a redeeming point — a redeeming point, certainly.

Charmed, my dear sir, charmed. Life here is an idyll — a perfect idyll.

Gently, dear boy, gently. Suavity, Harry, suavity.

Rent must be paid, dear boy. It is inevitable, Harry, inevitable.

True blue, Harry, true blue!

Shame, Harry, shame!

Not a doubt of it, my dear sir: not a doubt of it.

Shame, Harry, shame! Shame!

You have an untutored mind, Trench, an untutored mind.

The cumulative effect of these verbal triptychs is exaggerated somewhat when they are nested together in this fashion, but even in the text, where they are separated by other blocks of dialogue, they occur with sufficient frequency to give us a clear impression of Cokane as a chronic rattle-head. In his hands, language loses a large part of that seemingly unlimited plasticity which it normally exhibits, and becomes instead almost granitic, capable of being formed only into these uniform slabs. In these quirkish clusters of iteration, the vocal mechanism slips the cog which should link it to consciousness, and goes on spinning independently, a machine with no human agency to run it.

No one in the play makes any direct reference to these crotchets which clutter Cokane's discourse, but his friend Trench is finally driven to upbraid him for another stylistic mannerism closely related to them. Cokane is excessively partial to foreign-language phrases and flourishes them with pedantic regularity. On occasion, the favored expression is fitted into a series like the ones already noted. Thus we have: "*Négligé*, my dear fellow, *négligé*," and "Too *dégagé*, Mr. Sartorius, too *dégagé*." At other times, the French or Latin idiom also forms part of a repetition, but instead of being repeated itself, functions as the equivalent of an English expression, as in: "Delicacy, Harry, delicacy! Good taste! *Savoir faire*!," or "Gently, my dear sir. Gently, Harry, dear boy. *Suaviter in modo: fort–*." Trench interrupts this last excursion, apparently suppressing temporarily the rebuke he is later to deliver.

That rebuke occurs in Act III, at a point when we have all but heard the last of Cokane. Sartorius has observed that whatever the outcome of the speculative venture he and Lickcheese are contemplating, Trench, as mortgagee of the properties involved, will expect his seven per cent as usual. To this Trench replies: "A man must live," and Cokane answers him with "*Je n'en vois pas la nécessité*." "Shut up, Billy," says Trench, "or else speak some language you understand."

Trench's strong reproof might with some justification be applied to Cokane's handling of English as well. If he does not fail to "understand the language," in the usual sense of that phrase, he does fail to comprehend, or does not take sufficiently into account, the necessity for a vital relationship between words and thought. For Cokane, words are little more than sounds, sounds which he enjoys producing indiscriminately, with cavalier disregard for the requirements of communication. A rather striking revelation of this tendency occurs in a line which accompanies one of the repetition series already quoted. The more complete speech runs: "*Négligé*, my dear fellow, *négligé*. On the steamboat a little *négligé* was quite *en régle*; but here, in this hotel, some of them are sure to dress for dinner." In the phrase, "a little *négligé*," the forced conjunction of English and French calls disproportionate attention to "*négligé*" as a word, as a sound; the word ceases almost to point to the real quality for which it ought to function as merely the symbol, and takes on a life of its own; its referent drops from view, because for Cokane it scarcely has a referent, or needs one. In much the same way, lines such as "Shame, Harry, shame," and "Finished, dear boy, finished," represent a departure from the norm of properly human speech.

These oddities of usage make the character a very special sort of eccentric, comic in himself, but not pointedly representative of mankind at large. On the other hand, a degree of relevance to a conspicuous, if relatively small, group of human beings found outside the theatre, does seem to be present. There is a meaningful parallel between Cokane's speech style and another important aspect of his character, and that other aspect in turn links the character unmistakeably to certain real-life counterparts.

Cokane is an aristocrat and self-appointed watchdog of the mores of his class. The unbuttoned social posture of his friend Trench keeps him in a persistent dither, with the result that very nearly the whole of his action in the play consists of expostulating with Trench for his failure to observe "the usages of society." Most particularly, he supervises every step of Trench's courtship of Blanche, instructing him, with all the fluttering solicitation of a dowager aunt, in the nuances of genteel orthodoxy. The following exchange is typical:

COKANE. Her father seems to be a perfect gentleman. I obtained the privilege of his acquaintance: I introduced you: I allowed him to believe that he might leave his daughter in your charge with absolute confidence. And what did I see on our return? what did her father see? Oh, Trench, Trench! No, my dear fellow, no, no. Bad taste, Harry, bad form!

TRENCH. Stuff! There was nothing to see.

COKANE. Nothing to see! She, a perfect lady, a person of the highest breeding, actually in your arms; and you say there was nothing to see! with a waiter there actually ringing a heavy bell to call attention to his presence! [*Lecturing him with redoubled severity*] Have you no principles, Trench? Have you no religious convictions?

At moments like these, and they occur throughout, Cokane is revealed as an unquestioning votary of the most hollow and artificial rituals of inherited privilege. His use of the imprecation "Bad form!" is quintessentially characteristic. For him, as for many of his class, "Follow the form and never mind the substance" is the first law of conduct. In this attitude toward social deportment we can detect a parallel with his stylistic manner; in both, the husk is preferred to the meat; the shell is valued though the life within has fled.

If this is true, then some degree of satiric point can be ascribed to Cokane's use of mechanistic utterance, and the character may be thought of as being at least moderately blameworthy.*

In other plays, Shaw uses the same device without satiric implications. Dolly and Philip, the twins who appear in *You Never Can Tell* (1896), are surely among the most endearing characters Shaw ever created.

Bergson points out that twins are comic in their very existence, since they represent a biological repetition; they allow us to laugh at Nature herself, caught in a moment of mechanical inflexibility. In creating Dolly and Philip, Shaw went considerably beyond what Nature does when it produces twins. Greatly elaborating upon the principle of sameness which twins naturally embody, he gives his fictional siblings a degree of identity for which life provides no models. Specifically, he gives them what amounts almost to interchangeable minds: whatever is in the consciousness of one seems to be simultaneously present in the consciousness of the other. At least this is true of that part of their shared consciousness which reveals itself in speech. The result is that they can each contribute alternatively to the vocalization of thoughts which they hold in common. Like a stereophonograph with faulty wiring, the flow of sound emanates now from one speaker, now from the other, but with such instantaneous interchange that not a phoneme is lost. They reveal this peculiar faculty shortly after their first appearance together.

---

* Though I have chosen to classify the speech of Sergius, Morell, Broadbent and others as linguistic satire, these characters might also be said to display linguistic automatism; the devices operate simultaneously. In the case of Sergius, for example, we laugh primarily at the artificiality of the language of romantic fiction (linguistic satire) but also at Sergius for his addiction to this language (automatism). In the case of Cokane and others to be mentioned here, the chief source of pleasure seems to be the addiction itself, and not so much the peculiarity of the style to which the characters are addicted. But the classification is nevertheless a bit arbitrary.

PHILIP. The fact is, Mr. Valentine, we are the children of the celebrated Mrs. Lanfrey Clandon, an authoress of great repute — in Madeira. No household is complete without her works. We came to England to get away from them. They are called the Twentieth Century Treatises.

DOLLY. Twentieth Century Cooking.

PHILIP. Twentieth Century Creeds.

DOLLY. Twentieth Century Clothing.

PHILIP. Twentieth Century Conduct.

DOLLY. Twentieth Century Children.

PHILIP. Twentieth Century Parents.

DOLLY. Cloth limp, half a dollar.

PHILIP. Or mounted on linen for hard family use, two dollars.

Admittedly, this performance is not much more than what we might expect from any two people who have had frequent occasion to report together on a particular subject, though, even at that, the statements follow one another with a machine-like rapidity and precision which is not ordinary in conversation.

But this is only the first, and least striking, display of the twin's facility for talking in tandem. In a later reference to one of their mother's hated books, they coordinate and consolidate their verbal efforts more closely still. When Mrs. Clandon refuses to tell them who their father was because they are "too young," they quote one of her own "principles" against her:

PHILIP. This is rather a startling departure from Twentieth Century principles.

DOLLY. [*quoting*] "Answer all your children's questions, and answer them truthfully, as soon as they are old enough to ask them." See Twentieth Century Motherhood—

PHILIP. Page one.

DOLLY. Chapter one.

PHILIP. Sentence one.

Another of their antiphonal chants also involves a quotation; this time they divide between them not the bibliographical data but the quotation itself. Philip is called upon to introduce himself to M'Comas and begins to do so, with the following result:

PHILIP. I was christened in a comparatively prosaic mood. My name is—

DOLLY. [*Completing his sentence for him declamatorily*] "Norval. On the Grampian hills"—

PHILIP. [*declaiming gravely*] "My father feeds his flock, a frugal swain"—

MRS. CLANDON [*remonstrating*] Dear, dear children: don't be silly.

Like two pistons driving a shaft, the twins "fire" here quite automatically and at perfectly regular intervals. The same little engine hums away for a longer space in a later scene. Again it is a quotation which sets the machinery going, but they soon leave that to alternate just as systematically on phrases of their own construction. They have just "come tearing in in their highest spirits" to have tea with their mother and to report to her on the progress of Gloria's romance with Valentine:

MRS. CLANDON [*anxiously, as she pours out his tea*] Phil: there is something the matter with Gloria. Has anything happened? [*Phil and Dolly look at one another and stifle a laugh*]. What is it?

PHILIP [*sitting down on her left*] Romeo —

DOLLY [*sitting down on her right*] — and Juliet.

PHILIP [*taking his cup of tea from Mrs. Clandon*] Yes, my dear mother: the old, old story. Dolly: dont take all the milk [*he deftly takes the jug from her*]. Yes: in the spring—

DOLLY. — a young man's fancy —

PHILIP. — lightly turns to — thank you [*to Mrs. Clandon who has passed the biscuits*]. — thoughts of love. It also occurs in the autumn. The young man in this case is —

DOLLY. Valentine.

PHILIP. And his fancy has turned to Gloria to the extent of —

DOLLY. — kissing her —

PHILIP. — on the terrace —

DOLLY. [*correcting him*] — on the lips, before everybody.

MRS. CLANDON [*incredulously*] Phil! Dolly! Are you joking? [*They shake their heads*] Did she allow it?

PHILIP. We waited to see him struck to earth by the lightning of her scorn; but —

DOLLY. — but he wasn't.

PHILIP. She appeared to like it.

DOLLY. As far as we could judge. [*Stopping Phil, who is about to pour out another cup*] No: youve sworn off two cups.

The kind of behavior exhibited in this and the earlier vignettes like it, may seem far removed from Cokane's tautologies, and there are, of course, important differences, but the same comic principle animates them both. It is again the familiar Bergsonian precept of "something mechanical encrusted on the living." What we normally expect of an individual's speech is that it shall assume configurations which are unique, discrete, and discontinuous, since speech should properly be the external sign of a consciousness which is unique, discrete, and discontinuous. True, the users of a given language all draw from a commonly held storehouse of words, and techniques for combining words into meaningful discourse, but within the limits of variability thus imposed, we expect and usually find an incidence of difference which comes very close to the less circumscribed incidence of difference in human consciousness itself.

Normally, then, no two individuals engaged in conversation with a third will direct their thoughts along lines so precisely similar as to produce a perfect semantic dovetailing of whatever fragments of their shared thought each chooses to verbalize. It is *possible*, of course, just as it is possible for a man to start a School For Wives, but it is unusual, and therefore the stuff of which comedy is made. It is unusual in the special sense that when two people begin to act in this way, each loses some part of that uniqueness which seems to characterize whatever is human, and takes on instead the aspect of a machine, which is expected to perform with perfect duplication of function.

Ordinarily, our laughter at a man who has "gone over" to the machines is markedly critical, as it is with Cokane. But Dolly and Philip escape our reproof, and for a very interesting reason. In most cases, an element of automatism in speech reflects some degree of automatism in thought. This is not true of the twins;

quite the contrary. Though their capability for assuming each other's communication tasks strongly suggests a mechanical element — like electronic backup systems — the burden of meaning they transmit is impulsive and spontaneous. They do not think and feel in standardized modules; the Life Force pulses as strongly within them as in any of Shaw's most febrile vitalists. Their total freedom from inhibition is nicely epitomized in one of Dolly's pert rejoinders:

CRAMPTON. So you want to know my age, do you? I'm fifty seven.

DOLLY. [*with conviction*] You look it.

It is true that Phil sometimes sounds a little like Cokane; he has a fixation on the phrase "my knowledge of human nature," and repeats it persistently:

No, Dolly: My knowledge of human nature confirms Mr. Valentine's judgment. He is right.

I doubt it. My knowledge of human nature leads me to believe that if he had a lot of money, he wouldn't have got rid of his affectionate family so easily.

Now my knowledge of human nature leads me to believe that we had a father, and that you probably know who he was.

But this is merely the quite forgivable affectation of a young man seeking credit for a larger endowment of worldly wisdom than he in fact possesses. It does not mar our dominant impression of Philip and his sister as two vigorous youngsters running rampant through the delicacies of Victorian convention.

In this respect, Shaw's delineation of Philip and Dolly represents an ingenious variation upon the familiar device of making characters talk like machines. Elsewhere, Shaw's use of the device is more orthodox. Such is the case with Cholly Lomax, of *Major Barbara* (1905).

Though he appears not at all in Act II, and remains on the sidelines in I and III, Lomax manages to use the expression "Oh I say," some fourteen times. Nor is this the only catchphrase to which he is addicted. The following lines occur directly following one another.

But really, don't you know! Oh I say!

Oh I say! Theres nothing to be exactly proud of, don't you know.

It must be a regular corker for him, don't you know.

No but look here don't you know — Oh I say!

Nobody'd know it, I assure you. You look all right, you know.*

 Still another phrase recurs with only slightly less frequency:

On the other hand, there may be a certain amount of tosh about the Salvation Army . . . .

Still, I have never shut my eyes to the fact that there is a certain amount of tosh about the Salvation army.

You are a very clearheaded brainy chap, Dolly; and it must have been apparent to you that there is a certain amount of tosh about . . .

 The fun of this series Shaw heightens by having Lady Britomart use the "tosh" line too, while she is in the process of deriding Lomax for his mangling of the art of communication.

 These examples represent Lomax's most overt parrotings, but he also demonstrates his incapacity for vital speech by his near-total slavery to slang and cliché. He freights his every statement with such dead weight as "old man," "chap," "ripping," "jolly good," "chucked," "corker," "and all that," and numerous others. His mind stamps out sterotype phrases so handily that he can communicate only by stringing a series of them together; the result is usually vacuity, if not complete incoherence:

You must look at facts. Not that I would say a word in favor of anything wrong; but then, you see, all sorts of chaps are always doing all sorts of things; and we have to fit them in somehow, don't you know. What I mean is that you can't go cutting every-body; and that's about what it comes to. Perhaps I don't make myself clear.

 Elsewhere, he is scarcely more intelligible. In fact, Lomax very nearly manages to *say* absolutely nothing, despite the number of times he opens his mouth and makes sounds. His speeches read like a list of idioms in an English Language drillbook.

---

* I have omitted only one short line, which occurs between the first and second of those quoted.

He suffers from an advanced case of linguistic automatism. He has all but lost the faculty for confrontation of objective reality through the medium of words. Stimulus produces direct response, without an intermediate engagement of consciousness.

Lomax represents such an extreme case that Shaw can hardly have intended serious social criticism in his characterization; few spectators will hear themselves in Cholly's speeches. True, the components of his style are easily recognized and assigned to a specific class of a specific society, but so outlandish is Cholly's entanglement in them that he seems rather a freakish individual than a representative of group aberrations. Moreover, his folly proves so harmless, so peripheral in the context of the action, that it provokes little more than amused indulgence.

In this, Cholly resembles Shaw's next chatterer, Sir Ralph Bloomfield Bonington, of *The Doctor's Dilemma* (1906). A thorough-going eccentric, "B. B." has a magazine full of cherished phrases and favorite tricks of syntax. One such stands out above all the others:

There is at bottom only one genuinely scientific treatment for all diseases, and that is to stimulate the phagocytes. Stimulate the phagocytes.

What is the real work of the antitoxin? Simply to stimulate the phagocytes. Very well. But so long as you stimulate the phagocytes, what does it matter . . . .

To me you are simply a field of battle in which an invading army of tubercle bacilli struggles with a patriotic force of phagocytes. Having made a promise to your wife to stimulate those phagocytes, I will stimulate them.

And these lines represent only a portion of the times he uses the incantation.

Another curious habit involves the restatement of a thought for each person present:

Theres a problem for you, Ridgeon. Think, Sir Patrick. Reflect, Blenkinsop. Look at it without prejudice, Walpole.

Just consider, Ridgeon. Let me put it to you Paddy. Clear your mind of cant, Walpole.

Well, let us be honest. Tell the truth, Paddy. Dont be hypocritical, Ridgeon. Throw off the mask, Walpole.

Believe me, Paddy, we are all mortal. It is the common lot, Ridgeon. Say what you will, Walpole, Nature's debt must be paid.

But these two fixations hardly begin to exhaust his repertoire. Much like Cokane, he seems incapable of saying anything only once. Time and again his tongue sticks on a word, letting go only after two or three repetitions:

Not at all, not at all. Your own merit. Come! come! come! don't give way.

Quite right, quite right.

A privilege, a real privilege.

Certainly, c-e-r-tainly.

My dear lady; come come! come come! come come!

Pooh! Pooh, pooh!

Ah, well, perhaps, perhaps, perhaps.

Another of these concatenations is accompanied by a stage direction, the phrasing of which clearly attests deliberate artifice on Shaw's part:

G o o o o o o o o o d-night, Paddy. Bless you, dear old chap. Good-night. Good-night. Good-night. Good-night. [*He good-nights himself into the hotel.*]

On one occasion, he repeats, instead of a single word, a syntactical arrangement of noun and epithet:

Dee-lightful couple! Charming woman! Gifted lad! Remarkable talent! Graceful outlines! Perfect evening! Great success! Interesting case! Glorious night! Exquisite scenery! Capital dinner! Stimulating conversation! Restful outing! Good wine! Happy ending! Touching gratitude! Lucky Ridgeon —

Temporarily interrupted, he goes right back to this babble, breaking if off only for a second interruption.

In another performance similar to this one, the phrases do not quite so closely parallel one another, but the effect is substantially the same:

We shall begin stimulating the phagocytes on — on — probably on Tuesday next; but I will let you know. Depend on me; don't fret;

eat regularly; sleep well; keep your spirits up; keep the patient cheerful; hope for the best; no tonic like a charming woman; no medicine like cheerfulness; no resource like science; good-bye, good-bye, good-bye.

Seldom, if ever, has the mechanical in language been presented in such outrageous proportions. On the strength of these last two outbursts alone, B. B. might well be called the extreme example of this venerable technique of comic characterization. Word duplicates word and phrase, phrase, till the elements of reasoned discourse become as meaningless as the tick-tock of a metronome.

There is no very compelling reason to see in B. B.'s verbal antics much more than the piquantly comic derangement of a most singular man; B. B. is an original, almost a grotesque. But at least a hint of ridicule of the "quality he professes" is probably intended. Shaw's exasperation with the alleged lunacies of medical practice is well known; he gave vent to it not only in this play and its lengthy preface, but in numerous other places as well. It is therefore a matter of some significance that this particular word-machine has his shingle out in Harley Street.

The link between B. B.'s linguistic disorders and certain supposed follies of the medical profession as a whole, is not strongly forged in the play, but it is no less surely there. Near the very center of Shaw's assault on the doctors was his contention that they made outrageous claims to certainty in dealing with phenomena so replete with variables and unknowns that only the most diffident tentatives ought reasonably be applied to them. It is in this connection that B. B.'s curious stylistic mode represents a burlesque of the posture Shaw attributed to a great many of his character's real-life colleagues. B. B.'s gabble is distinguished by its failure to achieve any but the most tenuous relevance to the phenomena with which it is meant to deal. Whether he is talking about symptoms and cures or is engaged in relaxed social intercourse, he heaps up piles of words, not merely in rapturous ignorance of their unsuitability, but with supernatural serenity, convinced of the perfect adequacy of his responses (if one may speak of conviction in a man who has apparently not bothered for years to examine the meaning of his statements, or, indeed, to see to it that they have a meaning). If this is an accurate description of the impression B. B.'s redundancies make upon us, then this comic trait may be considered a palpable, if admittedly oblique, reference to a related habit of which Shaw accused many doctors: the habit of blithely accepting and acting upon — as though they were proven theorems — suppositions about the human organism and how to care for it which had little or no basis in demonstrable fact. Like B. B., Shaw would thus seem to be saying, many doctors needlessly chatter away, automatically repeating and administering their own or a colleague's favorite nostrums, with never a thought about the degree of their applicability to the phenomena at hand. Like their fictional counterpart, though of course less so, they are automatons, clanking through a fixed set of activities, verbal and otherwise, with only the slightest assist from an animating intelligence.

Only one other character need be included in this survey of Shaw's use of comic repetition. He is John Tarleton, Senior, of *Misalliance* (1910).

A self-taught intellectual, of sorts, with a fondness for polite disputation, Tarleton has fallen into the habit of buttressing his arguments with allusions to prominent authors of the past and present. Proud of the catholicity of his taste in literature, he carefully cites the source of each of his gleanings, goodnaturedly directing his antagonist to the same source. His knowledge of the important ideas to be found in the great books of Western Civilization approaches the encyclopedic, and like the compiler of an encyclopedia he has composed a précis of each idea and filed it away separately in his head, with the author duly noted. He thus functions as a sort of computerized Digest of Western Literature, delivering up the desired data on demand, every item uniformly encapsulated in preformed syntactical structures.

Tarleton begins to demonstrate his capability for instant information-retrieval a few lines after his first entrance. In a discussion with Bentley about the nature of old age, Tarleton has pointed to his own wrinkles and grey hair and Bentley has called them "Jolly nice and venerable;" Tarleton replies: "Nice? Not a bit of it. Venerable? Venerable be blowed! Read your Darwin, my boy. Read your Weismann."

The last two lines of this speech begin a pattern to which Tarleton adheres, with sustained comic effectiveness, throughout the play. The admonition, "Read your ————— (Name of Author)," or some slight variation of it, is for Tarleton a quite irresistible stratagem, one which he must employ in all of his numerous debates. The refrain pops up at the end of his every rebuttal as inevitably as a jack-in-the-box:

Joy of life. Read Ibsen.

Paradoxes are the only truths. Read Chesterton.

Still, Democracy's all right, you know. Read Mill. Read Jefferson.

No. Wrong principle. You want to remember. Read Kipling. "Lest we forget."

Prometheus was chained to his rock: read Shelley: read Mrs. Browning.

Besides, why should I give way to morbid introspection? It's a kind of madness. Read Lombroso.

Yes, shyness. Read Dickens.

I'm for the Parliament of man, the federation of the world. Read Tennyson.

But I've a superabundance of vitality. Read Pepys' diary.

Our whole civilization is a denial of it. Read Walt Whitman.

Aware that an obvious device of this type can eventually begin to pall, Shaw takes care to forestall weariness by occasionally altering the basic form:

Still you know, the superman may come. The superman's an idea. I believe in ideas. Read Whatshisname.

Well, sufficient unto the day is the evil thereof. Read the old book.

Once, Tarleton is even caught short; "That's an idea, certainly. I don't think anybody has ever written about that."

In giving Tarleton this classic bit of comic "business," the recurring phrase, Shaw accomplishes at least two very important artistic purposes. *Misalliance* is among the most rambling and digressive of all his plays and there can be little doubt that its discursiveness is deliberate; Shaw had already demonstrated his mastery of more orthodox playcraft in such "action-packed" plays as *Arms and the Man* and *The Devil's Disciple*. But if he allowed himself to be quite blatantly talky on this occasion, he had by no means lost sight of the necessity for old-fashioned theatricality. For all its meandering loquaciousness, the play is regularly enlivened by interludes of traditional tomfoolery. The crash of Lina Szczepanowska's plane through the greenhouse roof, and Gunner's eavesdropping in the Turkish bath, are but two examples. Tarleton's broadly comic verbal habits function in much the same way as these other low comic incidents; they very effectively relieve what might otherwise have been rather tiresome disquisition. The comic tone Tarleton repeatedly establishes is especially helpful in this way, since it appears not between protracted debates but in their very course, as an organic part of them. Viewed in this way, Tarleton's repetitions illustrate Shaw's skill at fusing materials which are largely non-theatrical with others of proven comic power. Working in this way he is able to make not only palatable but thoroughly delightful the wide-ranging discussion which is the real substance of the play.

Shaw also elevates the stock device of the recurring phrase into a thoroughly credible personality trait, one which takes its place beside other traits to make Tarleton a convincing, three-dimensional character. Instead of allowing the earmarking phrase to carry the full weight of characterization, Shaw imbeds it in a matrix of related details which together give Tarleton a full measure of psychological reality. The result is that we never view the repetitions as a comic maneuver laid on by the playwright (though, of course, they are that), but as the natural outcroppings of a quaint personality. As such, they compare with Dickens' celebrated "Barkis is willin'" or O'Casey's "Darlin' man," "Darlin' funeral," "Darlin' book" sequence.

It is a measure of Shaw's confidence, not to say boldness, that he gives the habit not to a complete automaton, like Cokane, but to another of his vitalists. Though essentially mechanical itself, the trick of iteration is in this instance only a minor comic flaw in an otherwise healthy personality; enough has already been said about his incisive criticism of Gunner's affectations to illustrate Tarleton's general adherence to the dictates of good sense.

Shaw makes incidental reference to mechanical utterance in a number of other places, but his representation of it as a distinguishing mark of character is confined to these examples. Considering the close connection between the device and Shaw's program of ridicule of everything intractable and obdurate, its appearance is surprisingly infrequent. It may very well be that Shaw limits its use lest he himself be found guilty of the very sort of addiction he is criticizing.

* * *

Ronald Peacock has observed that "... no writer of stage comedy, not even Molière, can afford to neglect any source of amusement, and Shaw has the good sense to be as small on occasion as his greatest predecessor."[8] This statement might apply to a number of features of Shaw's comedies, but to none more aptly than his use of word-play.

In adopting this device, Shaw had not only Molière for a precedent but the other great comic dramatists as well; puns and other strictly verbal jests occur with great frequency in the plays of Plautus and Terence, and Shakespeare seems to have found word-play well nigh irresistible.

Despite such an illustrious heritage, the pun has long been held in popular contempt as "the lowest form of humor," a phenomenon which has lead, according to Max Eastman, to the enjoyment of puns not for their excellence but for their very badness. "The idea of this procedure," writes Eastman, "seems to be that if you can not enjoy a pun as a good joke, you may at least, regarding jokes for a moment as serious creations, take its very badness playfully and laugh. A bad practical joke thus becomes a ludicrous object of contemplation."[9] Shaw seems to have had something of this sort in mind with a number of his more "atrocious"[10] wrenchings of meanings.

But before looking at examples of this and other uses of the pun in Shaw's plays, it may be well to make clear precisely what is meant by this term. Under the heading "Puns, Jests, and Double Meanings," in his exhaustive study of Roman Comedy, Duckworth distinguishes "two basic types of verbal wit: (1) *equivoca*, or ambiguities: we expect a word to mean one thing and we suddenly discover that it means something else; (2) paronomasia, or word-play: we find, by the side of one word or in place of it, another word of similar sound used to produce a ludicrous contrast in meaning. Examples of both categories are usually termed 'puns,' since we have, in the one case, a different application of the same word and, in the other, two words of different meaning but of the same or similar sound."[11]

Addressing himself to this same question of terminology and classification, Freud calls only paronomasia puns, designating Duckworth's first class, *equivoca*, as "play on words."[12] In the following remarks, I shall use "pun" and "word-play" interchangeably to designate either class.

Puns involving mere similarity of sound are extremely rare in Shaw, and where they occur they are usually of the atrocious variety, rather obviously intended to provoke laughter by their outrageousness. Thus, in *Too True To Be Good* (1931), we have:

MRS. MOPPLY: Do you know that I have killed two of my children because they told me that? My own children! Murdered them, just!

THE ELDER: Medea! Medea!

MRS. MOPPLY: It isn't an idea: it's the truth.

The Fascinating Foundling (1909) contains a similar example:

ANASTASIA: Thanks. And now will you be good enough to tell Sir Cardonius Boshington that Miss Anastasia Vulliamy wishes to see him.

MERCER: Miss Anaesthesia Vulliamy, my lord, to see you.

A somewhat more subtle example from *In Good King Charles's Golden Days* (1939), demands a knowledge of French:

LOUISE: What you were saying about little kings and queens being everywhere was very true. You are very spiritual.

BARBARA: Ha ha! Ha ha ha! He Spiritual.

LOUISE: Clever, you call it. I am always in trouble with my English.

In a sense of course, these are not puns at all, for as Eastman observes, "A pun is generally thought of as a perpetration, rather than a mistake."[13] But though these are mistakes on the part of the characters, for the playwright they are perpetrations and the effect is much the same.

Puns built upon a double application of the same word appear much more frequently in the plays. The following exchange, from *John Bull's Other Island*, illustrates Shaw's usual method of employing this device:

BROADBENT: I want you to be rather particular as to how you treat the people here.

HODSON: I haven't treated any of 'em yet, sir. If I was to accept all the treats they offer me, I shouldn't be able to stand at this present moment, sir.

This process of having one character introduce a term and another repeat it with a different meaning occurs also in *Too True To Be Good*:

TALLBOYS: I should have become a drunkard had it not been for the colors.

THE SERGEANT: Ah yes, sir, the colors. The fear of disgracing them has kept me off the drink many a time.

TALLBOYS: Man, I do not mean the regimental colors, but the watercolors.

This example represents a slight variation of the technique of the first, in that the joke does not emerge until the character who introduced the term makes a second statement revealing his original meaning. But elsewhere in the same play, Shaw uses the more concise formula:

THE SERGEANT: You see, I'm in a mess.

SWEETIE: Well, of course, You're in the sergeant's mess.

Each of these jests hinges upon a single word; sometimes Shaw does much the same thing with a phrase, as in the following, from *A Village Wooing* (1933):

A.: That sounds literary. Was your father a man of letters?

Z.: Yes: I should think he was. A postman.

In none of these cases does the playwright make completely clear whether the pun comes about as the result of a mistake or through conscious artifice, though with the possible exception of the "mess" joke, all seem to be of the mistake variety.* In other instances, the character seems aware of the jest, as in the following, from *On The Rocks*:

SIR ARTHUR: Of course, I shall have to go somewhere for a rest; and if you could really recommend it as a bracing place—

THE LADY: Bracing? What for?

SIR ARTHUR: Well, bracing, you know. Bracing.

THE LADY: Curious, how idle people are always clamoring to be braced! Like trousers.

All of these specimens constitute what Freud would classify as "true double meaning," cases where a single word has two completely independent denotations. In a manner of speaking, such jokes actually employ two separate words which happen to have identical spelling.

Freud differentiates this group of puns from another involving proper names which also have "verbal significance." The example he gives, "Discharge thyself of our company, Pistol," (Henry IV, Act II.) has a parallel in *King Charles:*

BARBARA: If you mean clever, he is as clever as fifty foxes.

FOX: He may be fifty times as clever as I . . . .

A proper name also permits word-play in *Arms and The Man* where Raina announces that she is a Petkoff and the sleepy Bluntschli answers "A pet what?"** Moreover, Bluntschli's name is itself a pun, like that of a great many of Shaw's characters.†

Still another variety of double meaning exploits those words used in both a metaphorical and a literal sense. Freud offers this

---

* This distinction corresponds to the familiar distinction between witty and humorous utterance; most of Shaw's puns are of the humorous type.

**The line does not appear in early editions; it was probably inserted in the 1926 copyright revision. See the Penguin edition, 1952.

† Nethercot provides an analysis of most of these in an appendix to *Men and Supermen,* entitled "What's in a Name?"

illustration: "A medical friend well known for his jokes once said to Arthur Schnitzler the dramatist: 'I'm not surprised that you've become a great writer. After all your father held a mirror up to his contemporaries.' The mirror which was handled by the dramatist's father, the famous Dr. Schnitzler, was the laryngoscope."[14] Shaw seems especially fond of this type of word-play and employs it more than any other. *King Charles* again offers quite a clear-cut example:

KNELLER: Can anyone here draw a line better than I?

CHARLES: Nobody here can draw a line at all, except the duchess of Cleveland, who draws a line at nothing.

Charles plays with words in this fashion with nearly sufficient frequency to warrant classification as a "punning" character. To his brother James, he says: "So, you are going to be the English Louis, the British Roi Soleil, the sun king. This is a deuced foggy climate for sun kings, Jamie." A little later in their protracted political discussion, Jamie sets up another jest for Charles:

JAMES: Psha! there is not a plot in the kingdom . . . that he is not at the bottom of.

CHARLES: He is not deep enough to be at the bottom of anything, Jamie.

This last should perhaps be called a double-pun, for it depends upon literal and metaphorical meanings for both "bottom" and "deep."

In a number of other plays, the facility for capitalizing on double meanings is less strictly confined to a single character. Thus, in *Overruled*, we have:

JUNO: Is that all? Oh, I can't believe that the voice of love has never thoroughly awakened you.

MRS. LUNN: No, it sends me to sleep.

And elsewhere:

MRS. JUNO: You always talked as if it were a matter of course. You spoke with the greatest contempt of men who didn't kick other men downstairs.

JUNO: Well, I can't kick Mr. Lunn downstairs. We're on the ground floor.

A somewhat more refined example occurs in *On The Rocks*, where Sir Arthur asks Miss Hanways to "remember occasionally" that he is "the leader of the House of Commons," and she replies: "Oh, what is the use of leading the House if it never goes anywhere?" Finally, an atrocious example from *Press Cuttings*:

MITCHENER: And the public thinks the lot of a commanding officer a happy one! Oh, if they could only see the seamy side of it.

MRS. FARRELL: If they could only see the seamy side of General Sandstone's uniform, where his flask rubs agen the buckle of his braces . . . .

Press Cuttings also contains puns a great deal like these but not strictly identical:

BALSQUITH: But you can't shoot them down! Women, you know!

MITCHENER: Yes, you can. Strange as it may seem to you as a civilian, Balsquith, if you point a rifle at a woman and fire it, she will drop exactly as a man drops.

The joke here depends upon a double meaning for the word "can;" Balsquith uses it quite loosely, to mean "ought" or "should" and though this cannot be called a metaphorical usage, it is sufficiently removed from the literal meaning of the word, i.e., absolute potentiality, to allow Mitchener to make a joke by interpreting the word quite literally. The case somewhat resembles what Freud describes as "the same words used in their full or watered-down meaning." [15] Analyzing this multiple use of the same material," Freud points out that "There are words which, when used in certain connections, have lost their original full meaning, but which regain it in other connections. A joke of Lichtenberg's," he continues, "carefully singles out circumstances in which the watered-down words are bound to regain their full meaning: " 'How are you getting along?' the blind man asked the lame man. 'As you see,' the lame man replied to the blind man." [16]

Thus, in *Press Cuttings*, we also find:

MITCHENER: [To his orderly, who has just entered his office.]
What do you want?
THE ORDERLY: I don't want anything, governor, thank you.
The secretary . . . . [Proceeds to deliver message.]
And again:
MITCHENER: Well, I'm dashed.
THE ORDERLY: Yes, sir.
MITCHENER: What do you mean by Yes, sir?
THE ORDERLY: Well, you said you was dashed, sir; and you did
look — if you'll excuse my saying it, sir — well, you looked it.

This process of taking literally words clearly intended to be interpreted otherwise, also figures rather prominently in *Major Barbara*. Lady Britomart is the chief practitioner and her two primary foils are Stephen and Lomax. Both these characters tend to use words in a fashion that has little to do with meaning. Accordingly, Shaw emphasizes this aspect of their speech habits by having Lady Britomart interpret certain of their utterances as though they really meant what they ought to mean. Thus, when Lomax throws out "Oh I say," as he does at every possible opportunity, she replies: "You are not called upon to say anything, Charles." Another time, with his usual devotion to slang, Charles asks: "I wonder how the old man will take it," to which Lady Brit replies: "Much as the old woman will, no doubt, Charles." "I didn't mean — at least —," Charles splutters, desperately trying to redeem himself. "You didn't think, Charles. You never do; and the result is, you never mean anything," Lady Brit replies.

With Stephen, she plays much the same game. Advised that she intends to invite Undershaft to the house, Stephen protests: "Ask him here! ! !" "Do not repeat my words, Stephen," she answers. "Where else can I ask him?" Earlier, asked for advice on how to provide dowries for his sisters, Stephen points out that he has "never interfered in the household—." Again Lady Brit twists his meaning and cuts him off with: "No: I should think not. I don't want you to order the dinner." In a similar exchange, she asks Stephen whether he is listening to her and he says: "Of course," whereupon she replies: "No: It's not of course. I want something much more than your everyday matter-of-course attention."

These examples show Lady Britomart's most characteristic brand of word-play, but at least once she adopts the metaphorical pun. As she is about to enter one of her husband's powder sheds, the attendant stops the group with: "You can't take anything explosive in here, sir." "What do you mean?" she asks. "Are you alluding to me?"

Lady Britomart has most of the play's verbal jests, but on one occasion, Undershaft mimics her way with words. Having just accepted a handsome contribution from Undershaft, Mrs. Baines exclaims: "Thank God!" "You don't thank me?" he asks.

Elsewhere Undershaft trifles with language in a way that cannot strictly be classified with double meanings, but which does involve word-play of a sort. "I wouldn't have your conscience, not for all your income," Peter Shirley proclaims. "I wouldn't have your income, not for all your conscience," says Undershaft. Later in the play, he repeats the trick with Lady Britomart. "What does it matter whether they are true if they are wrong?" she demands. "What does it matter whether they are wrong if they are true?" he answers.

Shaw had used precisely the same form some seven years before, in *Caesar and Cleopatra*:

POTHINUS: Caesar: I come to warn you of a danger, and to make you an offer.

CAESAR: Never mind the danger. Make the offer.

RUFIO: Never mind the offer. What's the danger?

He was also to use it again, more than once, during the next several years. In *The Interlude at The Playhouse* (1907):

THE MANAGER: [*Beginning his speech*] Dear friends — I wish I could call you ladies and gentlemen —

THE MANAGER'S WIFE: Hm! Hm! Hm!

THE MANAGER: What's the matter?

THE MANAGER'S WIFE: [*Prompting him*] Ladies and gentlemen, I wish I could call you dear friends.[17]

In *Overruled* (1912):

JUNO: . . . It doesn't matter about your conduct if your principles are all right.
GREGORY: Bosh! It doesn't matter about your principles if your conduct is all right.

The play here is not so much upon the meanings of words as upon word order. In each instance, certain key words in the initial statement are transposed and the statement repeated with the position of these words reversed. Ordinarily, such an arbitrary disruption of word order would result either in a corresponding disruption of meaning or in a simple restatement of the original meaning. "King live the long" would be an example of the first, "Dead is God" an example of the second. But here neither occurs. Instead, the restatement is both meaningful and the exact *opposite* of the original. Since it is highly unusual for this to occur, it represents a departure from one of the norms of language, just as the concurrence of two or more meanings in a single sound represents a departure from another norm.

This latter variety of departure occurs in another exchange which sounds like these transpositions but which really works on a different principle. In *Great Catherine* we hear:

EDSTASTON: . . . I am a Bachelor of Arts.
PATIOMKIN: It is enough that you are a bachelor, darling: Catherine will supply the arts.

The joke here takes the more familiar form of a double pun, one based on two meanings of "Bachelor," the other on two meanings of "Arts."

Double meanings are far and away Shaw's favorite style of word-play. The quoted examples of word-order transposition may very well constitute the full catalog of that type. Equally rare are examples of comically exaggerated alliteration, such as the following from *The Gospel of the Brothers Barnabas*:

THE PARLOR MAID: It would never have come into my head if you hadn't put it there, sir. Me and cook had a look at your book.
CONRAD: What!
    You and cook
    Had a look
    At my book!   [*Shaw's typography*]

This must be compared with a line in *As Far As Thought Can Reach*, spoken by Acis: "Cut the cackle; and come to the synthetic couple." In a similar vein, the Page in *Saint Joan* has "Pious Peter will have to pick a peck of pickled pepper." There are doubtless others, but certainly not many.

Even double meanings are relatively infrequent. Lady Britomart is the only character in a major play who equivocates on anything like a regular basis, and even in the lesser plays full-fledged punning characters are not at all usual. King Charles perhaps qualifies, but otherwise there is only Immenso Champernoon, of *A Glimpse Of The Domesticity Of Franklyn Barnabas.**

Conrad describes Immenso as "a pathological case." "There is a disease called echolalia," he continues. "It sets stupid people gabbling rhymes: that is, words that echo each other. Imm here, being a clever chap, gabbles ideas that echo. He's by way of being a pundit, and is really only a punster." Immenso demonstrates the accuracy of this characterization in lines which immediately follow it:

IMMENSO: Be it so. You may say the same of Plato, of Shakespear. At all events, I keep to the point, which is the home.

FRANKLYN: Clara is the point.

IMMENSO: She is the point inasmuch as you have a tendency to stray from her. But the definition of a point is position without

---

* The text may be found in *Complete Plays With Prefaces*, II, xi-cliii. According to the editors of that collection, "*A Glimpse of the Domesticity of Franklyn Barnabas* was originally intended to be Act II of Part II in Back to Methuselah. It was withheld by Shaw from performance or publication with the play in 1921 and later published in Short Stories, Scraps and Shavings in 1932. It was first performed in New York in 1960" (p. cvii).

In a note on the play, written for the 1932 edition and reproduced in the 1962 edition, Shaw reveals that one of his reasons for at first withholding the piece from public view was that it contained an "inadequate and libellous" caricature of "a notable social philospher of our day," a man who "began without a figure as a convivial immensity with vine leaves in his hair . . . and in middle life slimmed into a Catholic saint." (p. cx). The original can only be G. K. Chesterton, an "immense" man, a famous convert to Catholicism and an accomplished punster. The name "Chester" derives from the Latin for "camp" and the suffix "-er," which denotes persons or things connected with something. The suffix "-ton" is a variation of the dialectal "tone," meaning "one." "Champ(s)" is French for "camp," from the same Latin root as "Chest-". The suffix "-oon" is Middle English for "one." Hence, "Champernoon" equal "Chesterton."

magnitude. Now Clara has both position and magnitude; and you will find that the more you attempt to destroy her position, the more oppressive her magnitude will become.

The puns employed here are reasonably subtle (or subtly reasonable) and as such embody a degree of rhetorical force. More often, Immenso's quiddities are of the more atrocious kind. Further along in their discussion of Franklyn's marital difficulties, Franklyn declares: "If I find married life with Clara intolerable, I shall chuck it and chuck her; and that's all about it." Immenso replies: "Many men begin by chucking the woman they love. The saying that 'each man slays the thing he loves' would be more true if it ran that 'each man chucks the thing he loves;' but he usually chucks it under the chin. In any other sense you will find it difficult to chuck Clara."

Franklyn's spat with Clara also provides Immenso with another opportunity of which he makes the very most. Conrad concludes that his brother and sister-in-law have reached a "stalemate" and Immenso quickly seizes upon the word and bats it about:

IMMENSO: Stalemate. That is exactly what is wrong with Frank.

FRANKLYN: What do you mean?

IMMENSO: My meaning is obvious. You are Clara's mate; and in the course of a too monotonous domestic routine you have become stale.

FRANKLYN: And Clara? Do you find her any fresher?

IMMENSO: Clara, with an instinct that amounts to genius, has recognized the situation. Finding herself stale, she takes herself off and then comes back and woos you afresh. What we have just witnessed here is a renewal of the honeymoon.

Conrad quite understandably greets this performance with "Tcha!" but Immenso is not to be stilled. He goes on to string together a set of puns which in number, complexity and general outrageousness recall some of the worst excesses of Shakespearean word-play:

Clara went away a stale mate, and returned a bride. Why don't you do the same, Frank? Why do you stick here in a groove, like a tram car? An Englishman's house is his castle; and when I am a frequent visitor it may be called the Elephant and Castle. But what is the Elephant and Castle? It is not a place at which tram cars stay: it is a point of continual departure and continual return. It is an ark which sends out doves every minute, and to which the doves return when the waters have abated. I shall write a book describing the adventures of a husband who leaves his wife every month only to return and woo her afresh, thus making himself a perpetual bridegroom, his wife a perpetual bride, and his life a perpetual honeymoon. Thus we reconcile the law of change and the irrevocable contract. Thus John Bull in his daily round of work, John Doin' as you may call him, becomes also Don Juan—

Further fancies are about to ensue when Franklyn cuts him off, to protest: "For heaven's sake, Imm, if you must make puns, make good ones." But Immenso neither desists nor improves. Clara bursts in at this point to announce that Campbell, the butler, whom she had gone out to question about the purchase of some grapes, "is thinking of turning Roman Catholic." This is cue enough from Immenso. "I suggest to you Clara," he says, "that Campbell's case is not a simple case of the grapes, but of the fox and the grapes. Now THE fox par excellence was George Fox the Quaker. A Roman Catholic fox is therefore an absurdity. Campbell should turn Quaker."

The play on "Fox," which Shaw was to repeat almost twenty years later in *Good King Charles*, is not the only pun in the play which occurs again elsewhere. Clara confesses that "when I read Lao-Tse and then try to read Imm's stuff afterwards it bores me to tears;" Immenso answers: "Lao-Tse, being only a sage, cannot draw tears. For that, you need sage and onions." Later in *Back to Methuselah*, in *The Thing Happens*, Burge-Lubin addresses Confucius as "illustrious Sage-&-Onions."

Clara calls Immenso's use of the "sage" pun "a silly joke." Silly it may be, along with the others, but Immenso is not just a silly man. Shaw uses the puns here in much the same way that he uses repetition in his characterization of Tarleton. Nearly the whole of *Domesticity* is taken up with a discussion of various aspects of marriage. As a major participant in that discussion, Immenso contributes an eloquent defense of the institution, along orthodox Christian lines. Far from destroying, or even damaging, the credibility of his arguments, Immenso's conceits greatly enhance it. Skill in punning, after all, is a mark of a certain kind of intellectual agility; it bespeaks a quick and keen mind. Immenso's puns thus enrich and enliven his arguments, insuring them not just a respectful hearing, but an actively interested one. Seldom has "the lowest form of humor" been found in such good company.*

Regrettably, Shaw's use of puns on the other occasions noted cannot be similarly praised. Some of the more jarring specimens might be excused on the ground that they are so bad they are good, but this subterfuge will not work for all, or even a significant number of the cases. More often than not, Shaw's word-play seems cumbersome, prolix and clumsy in execution. He requires such elaborate machinery to get his joke set up and explained, that much of the fun is dissipated. Often too, the puns seem much too obviously forced, as when they depend upon usages semantically possible but hardly probable. It is extremely unnatural, for example, for an artist, even an amateur artist, to speak of "the colors," as Tallboys does in the example already quoted. As a result, when the sergeant quite understandably interprets the words as a reference to the regimental colors, and we subsequently learn that Tallboys meant "watercolors," the hand of the dramatist shows so blatantly in the whole operation that the joke misfires.

But the most serious flaw in Shaw's puns is their lack of witty point. As Edmund Bergler says, "[A pun] may be mere word-play, in which case the result is no more than half-comical; it can be word-play combined with the technique of wit; in this case the result is usually memorable as well as witty. There is a wide gulf between the primitive and refined varieties." As an example of the refined variety, Bergler offers: "Success — is to get what you want; happiness — to want what you get," an observation which, he says, ". . . contains, behind its mask of word-similarity, deep and bitter wisdom."[18] Very little of Shaw's word-play will pass muster when this standard is applied. Undershaft's forays measure up and, just barely, some of Immenso's, but most of the puns are, in Bergler's terms, "no more than half-comical."

---

* His arguments are almost identical with those put forth by Chesterton in his book on Shaw, first published in 1909.

Eastman suggests quite a different criterion for a good pun. ". . . a double-meaninged word," he writes, "may conjure up two images in the imagination which violently refuse to mix. That is the funniest thing a pun can do . . . . And when it does that, it has no need of meaning."[19] Shaw fares rather better under this system of scoring; the "sage" pun and the "man of letters" pun, for example, would seem to meet Eastman's "double-image" requirement. But the criterion itself seems to me less satisfactory than Bergler's. Even if it is true, as is by no means certain, that the process Eastman describes is "the funniest thing a pun can do," we are left with a measuring stick of questionable utility. What is funniest in dramatic comedy cannot very well be made the major determinant of the worth of such works. Fancourt Babberly pouring tea into Spettigue's top hat has no doubt aroused greater laughter over the years than Mirabell and Millamant drawing up their curious marriage contract, but the relative positions of these two scenes on a scale of comic excellence is hardly in doubt. Congreve's creation gives us both fun *and* meaning, and the best puns, as Bergler suggests, do the same. Few of Shaw's double meanings give us a sufficient portion of the latter.

If this appraisal seems unduly harsh, one need only recall that most of the puns under discussion occur in Shaw's short plays, trivial pieces which he himself dismissed with subtitles such as "A disgrace to the Author," and "A Piece of Utter Nonsense." His word-play might be similarly described.

CHAPTER VI

The Neutral Voice

The techniques examined thus far show the nature and extent of Shaw's exploitation of the direct comic potentialities of words as words. These techniques account for a significant part of the comic power of both major and minor characters in a number of Shaw's more important plays. But there remain several characters whose speech exhibits none of the oddities of a Sergius or a Drinkwater, nor the penchant for punning of a Lady Britomart. Dick Dudgeon, Lady Cicely, Caesar, John Tanner, Undershaft and a number of their acquaintances, though principal agents in highly amusing plays, sport no quaint linguistic trappings whose cut and hue arouse mirth. The reason for this has already been indicated. Primarily interested in conflicts of ideas, with an unconventional thinker confronting and eventually converting a less enlightened opponent, Shaw needs for his vital character – his spokesman – a verbal instrument capable of expressing the subtleties of a fertile and agile mind, and for the antagonist a style of speech at least sufficiently normal to make probable his eventual disillusionment. Accordingly, Shaw's major characters exhibit either no linguistic aberrance at all or only so much as will not obviate a subsequent change to more acceptable patterns of behavior, as in the case of Sergius, Brassbound, Morell and Marchbanks, already noted.

Those agents whose speech is altogether free of ridiculous elements employ instead a style which may be described as neutral or transparent.[1] Unremarkable in itself, it forms a particularly apt medium through which may be viewed the myriad shifts of plot, character and thought; it does *not* constitute an object offered for inspection and amused contemplation on its own account. Here we laugh at what is said, rather than the manner of expression.

But as already indicated, the manner of expression may contribute indirectly to comic power, by virtue of the effectiveness with which it functions as an instrument of disclosure. Accordingly, we need to consider certain characteristics of this neutral style, noting their special efficacy as the media of comic representation.

Jonas Barish has said that, "Stylistic studies would seem to need an approach located somewhere between two pillars of unwisdom, between extreme statistic-hunting on the one hand and rank impressionism on the other, one that accepts the subjective basis for judgments of style but places this under conditions of maximum control."[2] Impressionistic accounts of Shaw's way with stage dialogue appear wherever his plays receive critical attention, though they usually amount to little more than passing comments in books and essays primarily concerned with other aspects of Shaw's dramaturgy. J. C. Trewin speaks of the "prickling, leaping wit of Shaw," and calls his dialogue "a union of steel and shot-silk . . . admirably speakable . . . [its] long sentences . . . balanced to a hair."[3] Bentley praises "the swift tempo, the sudden and unexpected reverses (especially anticlimaxes), in a phrase, the unusual energy coupled with the unusual intellect."[4] Elsewhere he calls the "athleticism and vitality" of Shaw's "simple prose," "unique in literature," in point of quality. "Splendid in itself," he concludes, "this mode of utterance is especially splendid for comedy."[5] Moody Prior finds in Shaw's diction an "inexhaustible effervescence [and] vitality,"[6] while Priestley points to its "hammering, smashing,"[7] tone. Noting the same aspects as Priestley but voicing more displeasure with them, Max Beerbohm writes: "In [Shaw's] plays, I really enjoy only his stage directions; the dialogue is vortical and, I find, fatiguing. It is like being harangued; it is like being a member of one of those crowds he used to exhort on street corners. He uses the English language like a truncheon. It is an instrument of attack, don't you know. No light and shade, no poetry."[8] In a rare comment on Shaw's work, Eliot seems to echo Beerbohm, calling Shaw "poetically less than immature."[9]

Such comments provide valuable clues to the nature of Shaw's non-eccentric dramatic dialogue, but their highly metaphorical character demands supplementation by concrete analysis and literal description. Though the remarks of these critics probably escape the charge of "rank impressionism," they need to be tested by the identification and examination of the actual linguistic components of the style they seek to describe. If, for example, Shaw's dialogue has a quality called "effervescence," it should be possible to show in what elements of vocabulary and syntax that quality inheres, or through what process of stylistic maneuvering the quality has been achieved.*

Shaw has himself provided important clues. In the preface to *Immaturity* he describes the kind of style he sought and his reason for seeking it:

I have never aimed at style in my life: style is a sort of melody that comes into my sentences by itself. If a writer says what he has to say as accurately and effectively as he can, his style will take care of itself, if he has a style. But I did set up one condition in my early days. I resolved that I would write nothing that should not be intelligible to a foreigner with a dictionary, like the French of Voltaire; and I therefore avoided idiom. (Later on I came to seek idiom as being the most highly vitalized form of language).[10]

* I first attempted to answer such questions in my dissertation, "Language and Laughter: A Study of Comic Diction in the Plays of Bernard Shaw" (Indiana University, 1961). In the following year, Richard M. Ohmann published his analysis of Shaw's non-dramatic prose, *Shaw: The Style and The Man* (Middletown, Connecticut, 1962). Several of Ohmann's conclusions about the style of Shaw's non-fiction works parallel my own findings, set down in this chapter, about the style of the plays.

The interest in idiomatic language revealed in the concluding parenthetical statement, finds fuller expression in another observation Shaw makes in the preface to *The Admirable Bashville*:

Then there are the people who do not . . . read anything at all, and consequently understand no English except modern vernacular English. This class is by no means a negligible one even in the theatre; for it includes a large body of intelligent manual and open air workers and sportsmen who, though after their day's exertions they fall asleep in less than a minute if they sit down with an open book in their hands, can be kept awake and alert very effectually in the theatre by a play. Only, it must be a play in the vernacular. Otherwise it does not exist for them except as an incomprehensible bore . . . . I myself . . . discarded my early very classical style for a vernacular one."[1 1]

Assuredly, what a writer says about his methods of work does not always represent an accurate account of what the work actually contains, but where such stated intentions can be shown to have found concrete realization in the actual work, they help to validate claims for the organic, as opposed to the accidental or tangential nature of the artist's methods. Since Shaw is on record as having deliberately sought idiomatic, vernacular usage, the presence of such elements in the plays would seem to point to conscious design and would suggest that Shaw found in these materials qualities necessary to his artistic purposes.

But even without such declarations of intention, the wide use of elements of ordinary speech could be shown to have an organic relationship to the most basic of Shaw's comic ends. The known capabilities of the language of "intelligent manual and open air workers" make that mode of utterance an apt tool, if not indeed an indispensable one, for a playwright with Shaw's consuming passion for the communication – to the masses – of revolutionary social and ethical thought. Shaw's clearly attested, fully documented view of drama as above all instructive, and his view of the "shop-girl" as representative of the class most in need of the kind of instruction he wished to dispense, made the employment of workaday speech almost a necessary condition of his success. His preoccupation with ideas – with the destruction,

through ridicule, of old ones and the promulgation of new —
demanded an instrument that would make abstraction compre-
hensible and palatable, if not to the lowest common denominator
of London society, at least to "the people who . . . do not read
anything at all . . . ."

The plays do, in fact, show a marked bias in favor of the plain
style and in light of what has just been said it seems reasonable to
count this feature among the linguistic elements contributing to
comic effectiveness in Shaw's dramatic works.

We have already had occasion to notice one example of Shaw's
command of the vernacular and the idiomatic in contrasting
Bluntschli's speech with the eccentric style employed by Sergius.
Other examples lie ready at hand. Here is Dick Dudgeon shatter-
ing Judith's illusions about the nature of his sacrifice:

If I said — to please you — that I did what I did ever so little for
your sake, I lied as men always lie to women. You know how
much I have lived with worthless men — aye, and worthless
women too. Well, they could all rise to some sort of goodness and
kindness when they were in love. That has taught me to set very
little store by the goodness that only comes out red hot. What I
did last night, I did in cold blood, caring not half so much for
your husband, or for you as I do for myself. I had no motive and
no interest: all I can tell you is that when it came to the point
whether I would take my neck out of the noose and put another
man's into it, I could not do it. I don't know why not: I see
myself as a fool for my pains; but I could not and I cannot. I have
been brought up standing by the law of my own nature; and I
may not go against it, gallows or no gallows. I should have done
the same for any other man in the town, or any other man's wife.
Do you understand that?

Several features of the passage deserve notice. Like Bluntschli,
Dudgeon uses contractions freely. He also employs with remarkable consistancy the word order most common to English:
subject, verb, object. Though most of his sentences are either
complex or compound, the various syntactical elements occupy
the positions usually assigned them in spoken English and the
more informal kinds of writing. Thus, in the line beginning "What
I did last night . . . ," he puts the participial modifier last rather

than first, where it would give the sentence a much more artificial cast. Also contributing to the artless, natural quality of the passage is the preponderance of Anglo-Saxon monosyllables. Finally, we may notice that Dick turns easily to a number of expressions which clearly belong to the most casual of styles: "set . . . store by," "red hot," "in cold blood," and "for my pains."

As everyday English parlance goes, none of these features is remarkable. And that is precisely the point here. Fowler defines "vernacular" as "the words that have been familiar to us as long as we can remember, the homely part of the language, in contrast with the terms that we have consciously acquired." "Idiom" he calls "the method of expression characteristic of or peculiar to the native speakers of a language; i.e., it is racy, or unaffected or natural English."[12]

Dudgeon's speech is thus not so much a style as the very negation of style, a confinement of language to its most characteristic, and hence least obtrusive configurations. As such, it has obvious drawbacks. It cannot, for example, achieve the heights of poetic expression which Beerbohm, Eliot and others seem to desire. But for Shaw's purposes it has distinct advantages. Not only do its comfortable familiarity and immediate intelligibility permit a ready grasp of the forces at work in the play, but its close similarity to real speech helps relate the thought of the play to the real world, thus assisting the spectator to make the intended applications. This the plain style does while preserving a raciness and vitality also appropriate to comedy.

Dudgeon's speech represents rather an extreme example of Shaw's use of the vernacular, but it would be a mistake to assume that what we have here is simply an isolated attempt at realistic characterization. As a citizen of an out-of-the-way hamlet in Colonial America, Dudgeon perhaps has a stronger claim on homely utterance than some of Shaw's other characters, but a canvass of the plays reveals that Shaw bestows this characteristic with little or no regard for the demands of verisimilitude. Thus, Caesar himself, in conference with the ministers of the Egyptian state, turns to the King's guardian and says, "Ah! That reminds me. I want some money." Elsewhere, he observes that "every dog has his day," praises some dates as "not bad," and describes one of Cleopatra's religious rituals as "hocus-pocus." In short Caesar's speech often displays the same simplicity and straightforwardness of vocabulary and syntax as Dudgeon's.

No less remarkably, Don Juan advises the lady Ana to "make the best of it," and the Prince of Darkness himself can speak quite knowingly of "a pretty kettle of fish." With equal ease, Undershaft counsels his son not to "rub it in," warns him on another occasion of being "blown to smithereens," and taunts Cusins with the accusation that his "grip is slipping."

To be sure, a phrase does not make a style and it would be inaccurate to say that these characters talk like shop-girls simply because they occasionally use such expressions. But the presence of these idioms and colloquialisms does serve to hold their speech close to that meridian line of vocal utterance which we call the vernacular.

Shaw keeps his dramatic dialogue close to the more familiar patterns of spoken English in another way as well. Considering the abstract nature of the topics which engage his characters' attention, there is a remarkable concreteness in their style of speech. Some of this can be seen in the features already noted. But it appears more particularly in the characters' habit of translating ideas into concrete terms by the use of analogy, simile and metaphor. These devices may seem strange allies of the vernacular, since we tend to associate them more often with an elevated style, but in point of fact they may be either elevated or homely, depending upon the qualities of the image they convey. "White as snow" is a simile after all, but its natural place in the vernacular is as well established as the place of "It wasn't me," "Who do you take me for?" and innumerable other idioms. Thus, by using figures which relate ideas to the familiar facts of everyday existence, Shaw manages to avail himself of certain of the tools of formal writing while still conveying the impression of spontaneous, unadorned speech. Witness the following, from *Major Barbara*; Undershaft is speaking:

Look at poor little Jenny Hill, the Salvation lassie! she would think you were laughing at her if you asked her to stand up in the street and teach grammar or geography or mathematics or even drawingroom dancing; but it never occurs to her to doubt that she can teach morals and religion. You are all alike, you respectable people. You can't tell me the bursting strain of a ten-inch gun, which is a very simple matter; but you all think you can tell me the bursting strain of a man under temptation; You daren't handle high explosive; but you're all ready to handle honesty and truth and justice and the whole duty of man, and kill one another at that game. What a country! What a world!

"Geography," "mathematics," "ten-inch guns" and "high explosive": these are terms that require no explanation. Fitting them into an analogy with "morals," "religion," "temptation," "honesty," "truth," and "justice," Shaw states his novel idea not only clearly and amusingly but with a homeliness of reference which makes his point seem almost a self-evident truth.

The same technique appears elsewhere with considerable frequency. The Devil explains the nature of the "great gulf fixed" between heaven and hell as follows:

The gulf is the difference between the angelic and the diabolic temperament. What more impassable gulf could you have? Think of what you have seen on earth. There is no physical gulf between the philosopher's classroom and the bull ring; but the bull fighters do not come to the classroom for all that. Have you ever been in the country where I have the largest following – England? There they have great racecourses, and also concert rooms where they play the classical compositions of . . . Mozart. Those who go to the racecourses can stay away from them and go to the classical concerts instead if they like: there is no law against it . . . . But do the lovers of racing desert their sport and flock to the concert room? Not they.

Beginning with the extremely nebulous concept of the "angelic and diabolic temperament," – a topic well calculated to drive those sportsmen Shaw mentions right back to their armchairs – The Devil is very soon talking about classrooms and bull rings, concert rooms and racecourses; in a very short time the sportsman is not only on familiar ground, but is laughing a little at himself and his fellows and, perhaps, learning a little.

Other examples of the same strong ties with the speech of informal discourse appear in the talk of virtually all of Shaw's major characters. To cite a few, Cusins says of Barbara that she "bought my soul like a flower at a street corner." Cleopatra tells

Pothinus: "Caesar will eat up you, and Achillas, and my brother, as a cat eats up mice." In a somewhat similar allusion, Tanner says of Ann that "we shall have no more control over her than a couple of mice over a cat." A few lines later, referring to Ann's trick of styling herself an orphan, he exclaims: "It's like hearing an ironclad talk about being at the mercy of the winds and waves." Further denigrating his unwelcome ward, he protests that he "might as well refuse to accept the embraces of a boa constrictor . . ." as refuse to accept Ann's guardianship.

In a number of ways then, Shaw contrives to keep the speech style of these characters rather strongly oriented toward the patterns of oral communication normally employed by reasonably literate people. In choosing words, he prefers the commonplace to the exotic; in matters of syntax, he chooses the simple constructions in preference to the more artifically contrived. He lards his sentences generously with idiomatic usage and even when he employs formal figures he keeps their terms familiar and concrete.

None of these stylistic features, of course, is in itself directly productive of comic pleasure, in the manner of Burgess' cockney or Sergius' floridity. On occasion, notably in *Caesar and Cleopatra*, the more pronounced evidences of modern informal speech may prove mildly amusing by virtue of their incongruousness in the historical setting of the play, but the instances are rare; for the most part, Caesar's speech simply sounds quite unobtrusively ordinary. Granting such slight exceptions, the vernacular character of Shaw's dialogue counts in the measure of his comic use of words simply as an apt tool for the representation of his particular materials of plot, character and thought. Given Shaw's purpose of ridiculing popular notions about social ethics, his use of idiomatic language may be viewed as a contributing factor in the successful realization of that purpose.

But identification of the homely elements in Shaw's noneccentric stage diction hardly represents a complete description of it. It seems valid to say that this diction has close ties with the vernacular, but it cannot be said to be purely and simply vernacular speech. Bentley, having described a passage from *Getting Married* as "very simple prose," quickly adds: "At least it *sounds* very simple, which is the important thing in the theatre."[13] Shaw makes his dialogue sound artless, by the methods just noted, but he does so without excluding altogether stylistic strategies of a somewhat more elaborate nature.

One of the more common of these is antithesis, a device for which Shaw shows a special fondness. Dudgeon offers a clear-cut example: "You are right; but I daresay your love helps him to be a good man, just as your hate helps me to be a bad one." Here the two opposed members appear in a single sentence, arranged in perfect symmetry on either side of the disjunctive element "just as." More frequently, the correspondence of elements is less complete and the point of disjunction less clearly marked. Where this happens, the style retains the force of the antithetical construction, while avoiding the sound of artificial manipulation, as in the following, also spoken by Dudgeon: "He wrung my heart by being a man. Need you tear it by being a woman?" This use of the full stop, in place of a conjunction, for the fulcrum, and the switch from the declarative to the interrogative mode, help disguise the neat pairing of "he wrung" with "you tear" and "by being a man" with "by being a woman."

At other times, there is a sharp division of clauses but the antithetic halves do not observe strict parison, as in Lady Cicely's: "You know, don't you, that if you don't like people you think of all the reasons for not helping them, and if you like them you think of all the opposite reasons." The sudden veering off from strict symmetry in the last two words greatly enhances the delicate touch of comic wisdom the line contains. The ease with which she abandons the structure she has erected reflects a kind of capriciousness which colors the observation, rescuing it from the pious sententiousness or cynicism a more orderly completion might have conveyed. By a similar departure from balanced syntax, Lady Britomart gives added force to a comic antithesis:

There is no moral question in the matter at all, Adolphus. You must simply sell cannons and weapons to people whose cause is right and just, and refuse them to foreigners and criminals.

In other cases, the contrast of terms remains relatively unobtrusive for other reasons. Cusins, for example, says: "But as to your Armorer's faith, if I take my neck out of the noose of my own morality I am not going to put it into the noose of yours." Here the very commonplace "noose" metaphor diverts attention from the careful opposition of ideas.

At times also, the antithesis may be tucked into two closely-fused subordinate clauses, completely independent of syntactical disjunction. Rufio says: "Clemency is very well for you; but what is it for your soldiers, who have to fight tomorrow the men you spared yesterday?"

But if Shaw most often keeps the figure modestly veiled, he can also parade it openly on occasion. There is no mistaking the hand of the resourceful stylist in the following speech of Don Juan, "No: you were fully and clearly warned. For your bad deeds, vicarious atonement, mercy without justice. For your good deeds, justice without mercy." But even these lines, though certainly mannered to a noticeable degree, retain a breath of spontaneity; the omission of subject and verb in the two antithetic elements gives them a fragmentary quality at least suggestive of the ellipses common to live utterance.

Somewhat further removed from the configurations of unstudied speech, are Caesar's heaped-up antitheses in his salutation to the Sphinx: "In the little world yonder, Sphinx, my place is as high as yours in this great desert; only I wander, and you sit still; I conquer, and you endure; I work and wonder, you watch and wait . . . ." The *number* of contrasted terms here certainly gives the address a contrived tone, but working against this force, tempering it, are the very simple components of the rhetorical scaffolding; the idiomatic "sit still," the equally familiar "watch and wait," the facetious use of the pseudo-poetic "yonder,"* and the jauntiness of the naked "Sphinx," (he might at least have said "*O* Sphinx"), all combine to pull the style of Ceasar's night prayer back toward the solid soil of prosaic discourse.

But in any case, this speech of Caesar's is exceptional. It transcends the level of perceptible verbal manipulation generally maintained elsewhere, not only in Caesar's other lines but in the

---

* For American audiences, "yonder" also has a rustic flavor which affects the speech.

dialogue of the other plays. Moreover, far from invalidating what
has been said about Shaw's relatively discreet use of antithesis,
the passage reinforces the point. For the confrontation of mighty
Caesar with the inscrutable Sphinx certainly warranted a free
exercise of stylistic virtuosity, and the significant fact is thus not
that Shaw did so much but that he did so little.
    The antithetical construction has a number of virtues which
makes it expressly suitable for dramatic comedy. Genung, listing
it among the "Figures That Promote Emphasis," writes:

The principal of contrast, on which antithesis is based, extends to
much broader relations than are indicated by mere verbal opposi-
tions and structure of clauses. Thought, incidents, characteristics,
are often prepared for or set off by something that presents a
striking contrast, and gives thus the lights and shades, the con-
tradictions and incongruities, that continually occur to excite
interest in real life. Antithesis in this broader signification is one
of the most spontaneous resources of literature.[14]

Further elucidating the essentially dramatic character of the
figure, especially when employed with sharp clausal disjunction,
Barish says that antithesis "pits each element rigidly against its
opposite and matches it fiercely with its partner, dividing and
binding in the same moment."[15]
    The wide use of the technique in Shaw's plays may therefore
be viewed as one of the sources of the "athleticism," "vitality,"
and "effervescence," so many of the critics find in the dialogue.
It is often said that Shaw proved that ideas themselves could be
dramatic; one of the ways in which he makes them so is by
causing concepts to square off and "go to buffets," in the manner
of two trim, finely matched pugilists. De-emphasizing external
action, Shaw sets up conflicts in the language itself, to rivet attention upon the dialogue of outwardly static scenes. The vernacular
elements of his style help to fix his comic ideas in a context of
real human affairs; the free employment of antitheses make the
ideas dramatic; the two work together to promote clarity, point
and interest.
    A third distinctive feature of Shaw's style is his frequent use of
anaphora, or the repetition of a word or words at the beginnings
of successive phrases, clauses, or sentences. In the following

example, John Tanner uses the scheme twice, first with "of" and then with "ashamed."

I know it, Ramsden. Yet even I cannot wholly conquer shame. We live in an atmosphere of shame. We are ashamed of everything that is real about us; ashamed of ourselves, of our relatives, of our incomes, of our accents, of our opinions, of our experience, just as we are ashamed of our naked skins. Good Lord, my dear Ramsden, we are ashamed to walk, ashamed to ride in an omnibus, ashamed to hire a hansom instead of keeping a carriage, ashamed of keeping one horse instead of two and a groom-gardener instead of a coachman and footman.

Sometimes the repeated word appears as the first unit in a series of precisely balanced parallel phrases. Don Juan has, "Man gives every reason for his conduct save one, every excuse for his crimes save one, every plea for his safety save one; and that one is cowardice." But more often, only the initial term recurs, as in Caesar's promise to send Antony to Cleopatra:

Come, Cleopatra: forgive me and bid me farewell; and I will send you a man, Roman from head to heel and Roman of the noblest; not old and ripe for the knife; not lean in the arms and cold in the heart; not hiding a bald head under his conqueror's laurels; not stooped with the weight of the world on his shoulders . . . .

Sometimes, the repeated word occurs with only one other term, as in The Devil's "I call on it to sympathize with joy, with love, with happiness, with beauty—." But it may also introduce a series of complete sentences or independent clauses; Tanner tells Ann: "I fought with boys I didn't hate; I lied about things I might just as well have told the truth about; I stole things I didn't want; I kissed little girls I didn't care for." There may even be anaphora within anaphora. Cusins tells "Father Undershaft":

You do not understand the Salvation Army. It is the army of joy, of love, of courage: it has banished the fear and remorse and despair of the old hell-ridden evangelical sects: it marches to fight the devil with trumpet and drum, with music and dancing, with banner and palm as becomes a sally from heaven by its happy garrison. It picks the waster out of the public house and makes a man of him: it finds a worm wriggling in a back kitchen, and lo! a woman!

On occasion it may greatly enhance a specific comic speech-action:

LADY BRITOMART: (*violently*). Don't dare call me Biddy. Charles Lomax: you are a fool. Adolphus Cusins: you are a Jesuit. Stephen: You are a prig. Barbara: you are a lunatic. Andrew: you are a vulgar tradesman. Now you all know my opinion; and my conscience is clear, at all events.

Quite often, Shaw uses the device in conjunction with antithesis:

DON JUAN: My dear Ana, you are silly. Do you suppose heaven is like earth, where people persuade themselves that what is done can be undone by repentance; that what is spoken can be unspoken by withdrawing it; that what is true can be annihilated by a general agreement to give it the lie?

But proliferation of such examples could continue interminably. They appear, it almost seems, on every other page of the plays. Whether simple or elaborate, whether used alone or in combination with other figures, whether comprised of only a few repetitions or several, the device bulks large in the linguistic stock-in-trade of Shaw's characters. For the most part, he uses it with restraint, allowing it to do its work and produce its effects without attracting notice. But in at least one instance, he gives his facility with it free exercise; the superlative virtuosity displayed in the passage demands its inclusion here as a final illustration of the technique. The speaker is again Don Juan, addressing The Devil.

Pooh! why should I be civil to them or to you? In this Palace of Lies a truth or two will not hurt you. Your friends are all the dullest dogs I know. They are not beautiful: they are only decorated. They are not clean: they are only shaved and starched. They are not dignified: they are only fashionably dressed. They are not educated: they are only college passmen. They are not religious: they are only pew renters. They are not moral: they are only conventional. They are not virtuous: they are only cowardly. They are not even vicious: they are only "frail."

The insertion of "even" in this last line and the use of the monosyllable "frail" in contrast to the polysyllables which follow "only" in the earlier pairs, break the relentless rhythm of the passage, giving the ear a brief respite at the midpoint of the speech. This moment of relaxation over, the rhythm resumes, quickly shifting to a faster pace with the omission of "they are" at the beginning of each member:

They are not artistic: they are only lascivious. They are not prosperous: they are only rich. They are not loyal, they are only servile; not dutiful, only sheepish; not public-spirited, only patriotic; not courageous, only quarrelsome; not determined, only obstinate; not masterful, only domineering; not self-controlled, only obtuse; not self-respecting, only vain; not kind, only sentimental; not social, only gregarious; not considerate, only polite; not intelligent, only opinionated; not progressive, only factious; not imaginative, only superstitious; not just, only vindictive; not generous, only propitiatory; not disciplined only cowed; and not truthful at all − liars every one of them, to the very backbone of their souls.

Not surprisingly, The Statue greets this performance with: "Your flow of words is simply amazing, Juan." The speech represents a *tour de force* which contrasts sharply with the rather subtle display Shaw makes of the same power on other occasions.

The skillful employment of anaphora gives Shaw's style a number of highly desirable qualities. Analyzing its use in a set of "that" clauses in one of Shaw's early speeches, Dixon Scott wrote: "[The passage] is nothing but a series of separate statements, but they are so socketed that the result is torrential: the sentence seems positively to go whipping through its supporting semicolons much as a telegraph wire does through the posts when you watch it racing past from a swift train."[16] The device in parts accounts for the "hammering, smashing" quality Priestley mentions and for the "vortical" aspect of which Beerbohm complains. But if it sometimes makes the spectator feel that he is being "harangued," it more often produces a "rapidity, poignancy, unanimity, promptness, [and] an exquisite timing and adjustment of . . . parts,"[17] which not only compel attention but please the ear.

Obviously, much more could be said about the neutral style of speech employed by the majority of Shaw's dramatic agents. But these three components − wide use of vernacular and idiomatic elements, of antithetical constructions, and of repetition — seem to be the most important. Together they give Shaw's non-eccentric dialogue its larger contours. Middleton Murry has said that "Whatever goes to make a man's writing recognizable is included in his style,"[18] and these three components are the most clearly recognizable in Shaw's case.

They are, moreover, the components which contribute most to the comic power of the plays. Though in no way comic in themselves, they serve Shaw's comic ends by promoting clarity, by helping to establish a "real world" context for Shaw's comic perceptions, by stating ideas dramatically, and more generally, by conveying a sense of vitality, of color, and of pace. They are, in short, precisely what we might expect from a man who declared: "Effectiveness of assertion is the alpha and omega of style."[19]

* * *

These comments on the neutral voice conclude what I believe to be an accurate and complete account of the ways in which Shaw uses language for comic effect. It should be clear from all that has been said — if not, indeed, from the brevity of the study — that the comic in words does not claim a large share of Shaw's attention. Of his entire gallery of memorable comic characters, only a handful exhibit bizarre speech as a vital part of their comic makeup. Of these, only Eliza, Sergius and Broadbent are central characters in major plays and Eliza loses her linguistic eccentricity halfway through the play. The speech of the other characters mentioned in the preceding pages represents only an occasional wave on an otherwise placid surface. Even Sergius, for all his verbal posturing, maintains strong ties with a normal mode of utterance.

Nor is there anything very remarkable in this. Of the great comic dramatists, only Jonson consistently uses outlandish speech as a major comic device. Aristophanes, Shakespeare, and Molière restrict linguistic portraiture to peripheral characters, when they use it at all. In adopting a similar practice, Shaw is thus in the great tradition. If he uses the device more sparingly then his predecessors, he nevertheless shows that he can wield it with considerable skill when he chooses.

Notes

CHAPTER I. INTRODUCTION: WORDS AS WORDS

1. George Bernard Shaw, "Back to Methuselah," *Prefaces by George Bernard Shaw* (London, 1934), p. 489.
2. John Gassner, "When Shaw Boiled the Pot," *The Theatre in Our Times* (New York, 1960), p. 165.
3. Eric Bentley, *Bernard Shaw: A Reconsideration* (Norfolk, Connecticut, 1947), p. 99.
4. Dixon Scott, "The Innocence of Bernard Shaw," *Men of Letters* (London, 1917), pp. 17-23. For some of Scott's conclusions, see *infra*, p. 161.
5. J. B. Priestley, "G. B. S. – Social Critic," *G. B. S. 90: Aspects of Bernard Shaw's Life and Work*, ed. S. Winsten (New York, 1946), p. 51.
6. (Middletown, Connecticut, 1962).
7. Elder Olson, "William Empson, Contemporary Criticism, and Poetic Diction," *Critics and Criticism*, ed. R. S. Crane, abridged ed. (Chicago, 1957), p. 34. For more on this subject, see also Olson's "Outline of Poetic Theory," in the same volume, pp. 3-23, and his *Tragedy and The Theory of Drama* (Detroit, Michigan, 1961), pp. 87-125.
8. Attributed to Shaw by Eric Bentley, in "The Making of a Dramatist (1892-1903)," *Tulane Drama Review*, V, Autumn (1960), p. 8.
9. R. S. Crane, "The Concept of Plot and the Plot of Tom Jones," *Critics and Criticism*, p. 66.
10. Olson, *Op. cit.,* p. 33.
11. *Ibid.*, p. 51.

CHAPTER II. SHAVIAN COMEDY: THE MAJOR ASPECTS

1. George Bernard Shaw, *Three Plays for Puritans*, 2nd. ed. (London, 1904), pp. xxii, xxiii.

2. Shaw, "Widowers' Houses," *Prefaces*, p. 668.
3. Archibald Henderson, *Table Talk of G.B.S.: Conversations on Things in General between George Bernard Shaw and his Biographer* (New York, 1934), p. 63
4. George Bernard Shaw, *The Quintessence of Ibsenism; Now Completed to the Death of Ibsen*, 3rd ed. (New York, n.d.) p. 184.
5. Shaw, "Mrs. Warren's Profession," *Prefaces*, p. 228.
6. Shaw, "Three Plays by Brieux," *Prefaces*, p. 205.
7. Quoted in, Archibald Henderson, *George Bernard Shaw: Man of the Century* (New York, 1956), pp. 528-9, note 8.
8. *Three Plays for Puritans*, p. xxii.
9. *Ibid.*, p. xvi.
10. *Ibid.*, p. xxvi.
11. G. K. Chesterton, *George Bernard Shaw*, (New York, 1956), p. 109.
12. Shaw, "The Irrational Knot," *Prefaces*, p. 656.
13. Shaw, "Three Plays by Brieux," *Prefaces*, p. 198.
14. Walter N. King, "The Rhetoric of Candida," *Modern Drama*, II (September, 1959), 73.
15. *Three Plays For Puritans*, p. xxxii.
16. Joseph Wood Krutch, "The Shavian Dilemma," *George Bernard Shaw: A Critical Survey*, ed. and with an intr. by Louis Kronenberger (New York, 1953), pp. 122, 23.
17. Edmund Wilson, "Bernard Shaw at Eighty," *George Bernard Shaw: A Critical Survey*, p. 143.
18. Shaw, *Saint Joan* (Baltimore, Maryland, 1951), p. 12.
19. Ronald Peacock, "Shaw," *The Poet in the Theatre* (New York, 1960), p. 91.
20. "Bernard Shaw at Eighty," pp. 143-4.
21. *Men and Supermen: The Shavian Portrait Gallery* (Cambridge, Massachusetts, 1954), p. 3.
22. *Quintessence*, p. 39.
23. *Ibid.*, p. 40.
24. Quoted in Nethercot, *Men and Supermen*, p. 4.
25. *Candida*, p. 74.
26. Bentley, *Bernard Shaw*, p. 107.
27. C. E. M. Joad, "Shaw's Philosophy," *Bernard Shaw: A Critical Survey*, pp. 188-9.
28. Shaw, *Prefaces*, p. 50.
29. Henri Bergson, *"Laughter," Comedy*, ed. and with an introduction and appendix by Wylie Sypher (Garden City, New York, 1956), *passim*.
30. Bergson, *Comedy* (New York, 1914), *passim*.
31. Bentley, *Bernard Shaw*, p. 108.
32. *Three Plays for Puritans*, p. xviii.
33. Bentley, *Bernard Shaw*, p. 108.
34. *Ibid.*, p. 110.
35. Chesterton, *Bernard Shaw*, p. 88. Emphasis supplied.
36. Jacques Barzun, "Bernard Shaw in Twilight," *George Bernard Shaw: A Critical Survey*, p. 171.

CHAPTER III. DIALECT AND COMIC EFFECT

1. For a complete account of the origins of English comic prose, see Jonas A. Barish, *Ben Jonson and the Language of Prose Comedy* (Cambridge, Massachusetts, 1960), pp. 1-40.
2. Barish, *op. cit.*, p. 296.
3. *Ben Jonson*, p. 275.
4. *The Cockney: A Survey of London Life and Language* (New York, 1953), p. 13ff.
5. Joseph Saxe, *Bernard Shaw's Phonetics: A Comparative Study of Cockney Sound-Changes* (London, 1936), p. 8.
6. "English and American Dialects," *Three Plays for Puritans*, p. 306.
7. James Sutherland, ed., "The Modern Cockney," *The Oxford Book of English Talk* (Oxford, 1953), p. 366.
8. "Dialects," p. 306.
9. For a thorough analysis of Shaw's phonetics, see Saxe, *Phonetics*.
10. *The Enjoyment of Laughter* (New York, 1936), pp. 132-3.
11. *Three Plays for Puritans*, p. 308.
12. See especially. C. E. Montague, "Some Plays of Mr. G. B. Shaw," *Dramatic Values* (London, 1931), pp. 75-77; and Walter N. King, "Candida," 71-83. Morell and Marchbanks will be discussed in Chapter IV.
13. *Three Plays For Puritans*, p. 312.
14. *Bernard Shaw*, p. 111.

CHAPTER IV. LINGUISTIC SATIRE

1. George Bernard Shaw, "The Admirable Bashville," *Prefaces*, p. 739.
2. V. C. Clinton-Baddeley, *The Burlesque Tradition in the English Theatre After 1660* (London, 1952), p. 136.
3. *Geneva, Cymbeline Refinished, & Good King Charles* (London, 1946), p. 136.
4. C. E. Montague, *Dramatic Values*, p.81.
5. *Overruled and The Dark Lady of the Sonnets* (London, 1939), p. 159. Emphasis supplied.
6. *Dramatic Values*, p. 76.
7. King, "Candida," p. 75.
8. *Ibid.*, p. 75.
9. *Ben Jonson*, p. 295.
10. *Bernard Shaw*, p. 111.
11. *Bernard Shaw*, p. 108ff.
12. *"Modernism" in Modern Drama* (Ithaca, New York, 1953), p. 62.
13. Plato, *Philebus*, in *Theories of Comedy*, ed. Paul Lauter (Garden City, New York, 1964), pp. 6,7.

CHAPTER V. AUTOMATISM AND WORD-PLAY

1. J. B. P. Molière, *The Misanthrope*, trans. Richard Wilbur (New York, 1954), p. 9.
2. "Frogs," *Five Comedies of Aristophanes*, trans. Benjamin Bickley Rogers (Garden City, N. Y., 1955), pp. 128-9.
3. "The Twin Menaechmi," *The Complete Roman Drama*, trans. Edward C. Weist and Richard W. Hyde, ed. George E. Duckworth (New York, 1942), I, 463-4.
4. George E. Duckworth, *The Nature of Roman Comedy: A Study in Popular Entertainment* (Princeton, New Jersey, 1952), p. 357.
5. For a full exposition of the mechanical theory, which underlies much of the material of this chapter, see Bergson, "Laughter," p. 107ff.
6. For a complete analysis, see Barish, *Ben Jonson*, p. 214ff.
7. Eugene Ionesco, "The Tragedy of Language," *Tulane Drama Review*, IV, Spring (1960), p. 13.
8. Peacock, *The Poet in the Theatre*, p. 92.
9. Eastman, *The Enjoyment of Laughter*, p. 117.
10. Eastman's word for puns so bad they are funny.
11. Duckworth, *Roman Comedy*, pp. 350-1.
12. Sigmund Freud, *Jokes and Their Relation to the Unconscious*, trans. James Strachey, in *The Standard Edition of the Complete Psychological Works of Sigmund Freud*, ed. James Strachey (New York, 1960) VIII, *passim.*
13. Eastman, p. 127.
14. Freud, *Jokes and the Unconscious*, pp. 36-37.
15. *Ibid.*, p. 35.
16. *Ibid.*, p. 34.
17. For the text of the play, see *Bernard Shaw: Complete Plays with Prefaces* (New York, 1962), VI, 281-90.
18. Edmund Bergler, *Laughter and The Sense of Humor* (New York, 1956), p. 119.
19. *The Enjoyment of Laughter*, p. 126.

CHAPTER VI. THE NEUTRAL VOICE

1. The terms and the concept are borrowed from Barish, *Ben Jonson*. See especially Chapter VII, p. 291ff.
2. *Ben Jonson*, p. 44.
3. "Shaw as a Wit," *G. B. S. 90*, pp. 161, 163.
4. *Bernard Shaw*, p. 116.
5. *Ibid.*, p. 130.
6. *The Language of Tragedy* (New York, 1947), p. 298.
7. J. B. Priestley, "G. B. S. – Social Critic," p. 51.

8. Quoted by S. N. Behrman, in *Portrait of Max* (New York, 1960), pp. 23-4.

9. T. S. Eliot, "A Dialogue on Dramatic Poetry," *Selected Essays 1917-1932* (New York, 1932), p. 38.

10. *Prefaces*, p. 645.

11. *Prefaces*, pp. 739-40.

12. H. W. Fowler, *A Dictionary of Modern English Usage* (Oxford, 1959).

13. *Bernard Shaw*, p. 130.

14. John F. Genung, *Practical Elements of Rhetoric* (Oxford, 1959), pp. 103-4.

15. *Ben Jonson*, p. 28.

16. *Men of Letters*, p. 21.

17. *Ibid.*, p. 22.

18. F. Middleton Murry, *The Problem of Style* (London, 1960), p. 5.

19. Shaw, Preface to "Man and Superman," *Prefaces*, p. 165.

Lists of Works Cited

Aristophanes. "Frogs." *Five Comedies of Aristophanes.* Tr. Benjamin Bickley Rogers. Garden City, New York: Doubleday, 1955.

Aristotle. "Poetics." *The Rhetoric and the Poetics of Aristotle.* Tr. Ingram Bywater. New York: Random House, 1954.

Bab, Julius, *Bernard Shaw.* Berlin: S. Fischer Verlag A. G., 1926.

Barish, Jonas. *Ben Jonson and the Language of Prose Comedy.* Cambridge, Massachusetts: Harvard University Press, 1960.

Barzun, Jacques. "Bernard Shaw in Twilight." *George Bernard Shaw: A Critical Survey.* Ed. Louis Kronenberger. New York: The World Publishing Company, 1953, 158-177.

Behrman, S. N. *Portrait of Max.* New York: Random House, 1960.

Bentley, Eric. *Bernard Shaw: A Reconsideration.* Norfolk, Connecticut: New Directions Books, 1947.

_____. "The Making of a Dramatist (1892-1903)." *Tulane Drama Review* (Autumn, 1960), 3-21.

Bergler, Edmund. *Laughter and the Sense of Humor.* New York: Intercontinental Medical Book Corp., 1956.

Bergson, Henri. "Laughter." *Comedy.* Ed. and with an Intr. and App. by Wylie Cypher. Garden City, New York: Doubleday, 1956, 61-190.

Chesterton, G. K. *George Bernard Shaw.* New York: Hill and Wang, 1956.

Clinton-Baddely, Victor Clinton. *The Burlesque Tradition in the English Theatre After 1660.* New York: British Book Centre, 1952.

Crane, R. S. "The Concept of Plot and the Plot of Tom Jones." *Critics and Criticism.* Abrdg. ed. Ed. R. S. Crane. Chicago: University of Chicago Press, 1957, 62-93.

Duckworth, George E. *The Nature of Roman Comedy: A Study in Popular Entertainment.* Princeton, New Jersey: Princeton University Press, 1952.

Eastman, Max. *The Enjoyment of Laughter.* New York: Simon and Schuster, 1936.

Eliot, T. S. "A Dialogue on Dramatic Poetry." *Selected Essays 1917-1932.* New York: Harcourt Brace, 1932.

Farrington, Conor. "The Language of Drama." *Tulane Drama Review* (Winter, 1960), 65-72.

Fowler, H. W. *A Dictionary of Modern English Usage.* Oxford: Clarendon Press, 1959.

Franklyn, Julian. *The Cockney: A Survey of London Life and Language.* New York: Macmillan, 1953.

Freud, Sigmund. *The Standard Edition of the Complete Psychological Works of Sigmund Freud.* Ed. James Strachey. 24 vols. New York: Macmillan, 1960.

Gassner, John. "When Shaw Boiled the Pot." *The Theatre in Our Times.* New York: Crown Publishers, 1954, 163-69.

Genung, John F. *Practical Elements of Rhetoric.* Boston: Ginn, 1887.

Henderson, Archibald. *George Bernard Shaw: Man of the Century.* New York: Appleton-Century-Crofts, 1956.

—————. *Table Talk of G. B. S.* New York: Harper, 1925.

Ionesco, Eugene. "The Tragedy of Language." *Tulane Drama Review* (Spring, 1960), 10-13.

Joad, C. E. M. "Shaw's Philosphy." *George Bernard Shaw: A Critical Survey.* Ed. Louis Kronenberger. New York: The World Publishing Compnay, 1953, 184-205.

King, Walter N. "The Rhetoric of Candida." *Modern Drama* (September, 1959), 71-83.

Krutch, Joseph Wood. "The Shavian Dilemma." *George Bernard Shaw: A Critical Survey.* Ed. Louis Kronenberger, New York: The World Publishing Company, 1953, 120-25.

Krutch, Joseph Wood. *"Modernism" In Modern Drama.* Ithaca, New York: Princeton Univ. Press, 1953.

Molière, J. B. P. *The Misanthrope.* Tr. Richard Wilbur. New York: Harcourt, Brace, 1955.

Montague, C. E. "Some Plays of Mr. G. B. Shaw." *Dramatic Values.* London: Chatto and Windus, 1931.

Murry, F. Middleton.*The Problem of Style.* London: Oxford University Press, 1960.

Nethercot, Arthur H. *Men and Supermen: The Shavian Portrait Gallery.* Cambridge: Harvard University Press, 1954.

Ohmann, Richard M. *Shaw: The Style and The Man.* Middletown, Conn.: Wesleyan Univ. Press, 1962.

Olson, Elder. "William Empson, Contemporary Criticism and Poetic Diction." *Critics and Criticism.* Abrgd. ed. Ed. R. S. Crane. Chicago: University of Chicago Press, 1957, 24-61.

Palmer, John. *Comedy.* London: M. Secker, 1914.

Peacock, Ronald. "Shaw." *The Poet in the Theatre.* New York: Hill and Wang, 1960, 86-93.

Plautus. "Twin Menaechmi." *The Complete Roman Drama.* 2 vols. Tr. Edward C. Weist and Richard W. Hyde. Ed. George E. Duckworth. New York: Random House, 1942, I, 440-486.

Priestley, J. B. "G. B. S. — Social Critic." *G. B. S. 90: Aspects of Bernard Shaw's Life and Work.* Ed. S. Winsten. New York: Hutchinson, 1946.

Prior, Moody. *The Language of Tragedy.* New York: Columbia University Press, 1947.

Saxe, Joseph. *Bernard Shaw's Phonetics: A Comparative Study of Cockney Sound-Changes.* London: Allen and Unwin, 1936.

Scott, Dixon. "The Innocence of Bernard Shaw." *Men of Letters.* 2nd. ed. London: Hodder and Stoughton, 1917.

Shaw, George Bernard. *Arms and the Man.* Baltimore, Maryland: Penguin Books, 1952.

——————. *Cashel Byron's Profession.* Leipzig: Bernard Tauchnitz, n. d.

——————. *Heartbreak House, Great Catherine and Playlets of the War.* New York: Brentano's, 1919.

——————. *In Good King Charles's Golden Days.* London: Constable, 1939.

——————. *John Bull's Other Island and Major Barbara.* New York: Brentano's, 1911.

——————. *Man and Superman.* New York:Brentano's,1905.

——————. *Misalliance, Fanny's First Play and The Dark Lady of the Sonnets.* New York: Brentano's, 1914.

—————————. *Overruled, and The Dark Lady of the Sonnets.* London: Constable, 1939.

—————————. *Plays Pleasant and Unpleasant.* 2 vols. New York: Brentano's, 1906.

—————————. *Prefaces by Bernard Shaw.* London: Constable, 1934.

—————————. *Pygmalion.* Baltimore, Maryland: Penguin Books, 1951.

—————————. *Saint Joan.* Baltimore, Maryland: Penguin Books, 1951.

—————————. *The Apple Cart.* London: Constable, 1930.

—————————. *The Doctor's Dilemma, Getting Married and The Shewing-up of Blanco Posnet.* New York: Brentano's, 1911.

—————————. *The Quintessence of Ibsenism: Now Completed To The Death of Ibsen.* 3rd. ed. New York: Hill and Wang, n. d.

—————————. *The Simpleton of the Unexpected Isles, The Six of Calais, The Millionairess.* New York: Dodd, Mead, 1936.

—————————. *Three Plays for Puritans.* 2nd ed. London: Grant Richards, 1904.

—————————. *Too True to be Good, Village Wooing and On The Rocks.* London: Constable, 1934.

—————————. *Translations and Tomfooleries.* In *The Collected Works of Bernard Shaw,* XVII. New York: Wm. H. Wise, 1930.

Sutherland, James Runcieman. "The Modern Cockney." *The Oxford Book of English Talk.* Oxford: Clarendon Press, 1953.

Trewin, J. C. "Shaw as a Wit." *G. B. S. 90: Aspets of Bernard Shaw's Life and Work.* Ed. S. Winsten. New York: Hutchinson, 1946.

Wilson, Edmund. "Bernard Shaw at Eighty." *George Bernard Shaw: A Critical Survey.* Ed. Louis Kronenberger. New York: The World Publishing Company, 1953, 126-152.

INDEX

[*173*]

DATE DUE